# ALCOHOLISM
## AND THE FAMILY

# ALCOHOLISM
## AND THE
# FAMILY

## GILDA BERGER

The Changing Family
**FRANKLIN WATTS**
New York ○ Chicago ○ London ○ Toronto ○ Sydney

Library of Congress Cataloging-in-Publication Data

Berger, Gilda.
Alcoholism and the family / Gilda Berger.
p.    cm. — (The Changing family)
Includes bibliographical references and index.
Summary: Provides facts about alcoholism and its impact on
families, as well as treatment and recovery programs.
ISBN 0-531-12548-3
1. Alcoholism—United States—Juvenile literature.   2. Alcoholics—
United States—Family relationships—Juvenile literature.
3. Alcoholism—United States—Prevention—Juvenile literature.
[1. Alcoholism.]   I. Title.   II. Series: Changing family (New York, N.Y.)
HV5066.B46   1993
362.29'23—dc20     93-10898 CIP AC

For Victoria.
With great affection
and admiration.

# CONTENTS

# ALCOHOLISM
## AND THE FAMILY

# 1

# ALCOHOLISM:
## THE FAMILY DISEASE

Did you know?

> o Twenty-eight million Americans grew up in families where one or both parents have alcoholism.[1]

> o Half the youngsters in the juvenile justice system come from alcoholic families.[2]

> o About two out of every five parents who abuse their children are alcoholics.[3]

??? 

## WHAT IS ALCOHOLISM?

Alcoholism is a condition in which individuals drink alcohol habitually and to excess. The drinkers continue to consume beer, wine, and whiskey even though this results in serious harm to their physical and mental health as well as damaging their family and school or work life.

Alcoholism does not necessarily mean getting drunk every day. Sometimes the drinking takes on a pattern:

Henry is sober all week long, but every weekend he drinks almost without stop, starting Friday night and not stopping until he passes out on Sunday night.

Every few months, Alan gets mad at his boss, quits his job, and drinks bottles of cheap wine until he collapses. He does this every day for a week or ten days. He then takes a few days to sober up and get a new job. For the next few months he does not drink at all—until he has a fight with his new boss and goes off on another drinking binge.

Mary's job takes her overseas every few weeks. When she is away, she drinks heavily every day. She often shows up at meetings smelling of liquor. At home, though, she only drinks when someone drops by for a visit.

Henry, Alan, Mary—they are all suffering from alcoholism.

The way drinkers behave when they are drinking is another indicator of alcoholism. Drinkers who embarrass themselves, abuse their families, get into fights, have car accidents, or pass out are suffering from alcoholism.

People who are alcohol-dependent do things when they are drunk that they would never think of doing when they are sober. Drunks have been known to drive at over 100 miles an hour, to take off their clothes in public places, to pick fights with policemen, even to play "chicken" with loaded guns—often with deadly consequences.

Many people with alcoholism are eager to function as good members of society, whether as parents, students, or workers. But alcohol often robs them of the ability to tell right from wrong, safe from dangerous, appropriate from inappropriate. It also makes it harder for them to think clearly and quickly, and to coordinate and control the movements of their body. Alcoholism actually prevents them from being the kind of people they want to be.

Consistent and continual use of alcohol has long been known to cause many diseases and disorders, including liver disease, cancer, and cardiovascular problems. But experts are now looking at other critical problems related to alcoholism—especially the many ways in which it can damage and disrupt family life.

## WHY IS ALCOHOLISM CALLED
## THE FAMILY DISEASE?

Alcoholism is a family disease because the entire family hurts when one or more members are alcohol dependent. A serious drinking problem can lead to economic insecurity, a loss of self-respect, psychological and emotional difficulties, and such problems as divorce, delinquency, crime, and suicide.

People with alcoholism are often part of family groups. They have young, teenage, or grown-up children; they have wives or husbands; they have brothers or sisters; they have parents and other relatives. A heavy drinker can take all the fun and joy out of family life and cause harmful effects that can last a lifetime.

Alcoholism disrupts the family's living patterns. The family has trouble paying bills when the alcoholic misses days at work or gets fired from a job. The spouse and children get caught up in lies and denials to cover up the alcoholic's drinking problem. The family is embarrassed and humiliated when friends and relatives avoid them, and they feel further isolated as they try to hide the secret of the alcoholism from others. To make matters even worse, the alcoholic's spouse and children may develop physical and emotional disorders of their own caused by the difficulties they endure.

A survey report, entitled "Exposure to Alcoholism in the Family: United States 1988," suggested that alcohol may be a major determining factor in premature widowhood due to the early death of the alcoholic. A study of women who had their first encounters with alcoholism and problem drinking through marriage showed that 38 percent had been married to an alcoholic, but only 12 percent were currently married to an alcoholic. The study concludes, "Although many marriages survive the effects of alcoholism, either because the alcoholic seeks help or the family accommodates to the alcoholic drinking, it is clear that a large number of marriages dissolve in the face of alcoholism.''[4]

Alcoholism also adversely affects the marriage partner in other ways. In the study cited above, about 55 percent of the separated or divorced adults reported that their initial exposure to alcoholism came through their spouses. But drinking patterns and problems were found to differ between husbands and wives. Forty-six percent of women were exposed to alcoholism through marriage, compared to 39 percent of men. Husbands who were heavy drinkers tended to have drinking, rather than abstaining, wives.

A family environment with alcoholism contributes to many kinds of alcohol-related problems. Most teenagers are introduced to alcohol at home, and drinking parents are more likely to have children who drink. Even the grandchildren of alcoholics are more apt to have problems with alcohol than grandchildren of nonalcoholics.

Some of the alcohol-related behaviors include crime and violence. Incest—sex between a parent and a child—and battering—physical abuse within a family—are also associated with alcoholism. An estimated 30 percent of cases of father–daughter incest and 75 percent of cases of domestic violence involve a family member who is an alcoholic.[5]

It is not surprising that survivors of incest and battering have higher rates of alcoholism than normal; it ranges from 40 to 60 percent.[6] Incest and battering victims often blame themselves for what has happened. Because they feel so guilty, ashamed, and helpless, they themselves may turn to drinking as a way to escape the pain.

William L. Roper, M.D., director of the Centers for Disease Control, described alcoholism as a family disease this way: ''Not only are family members of alcoholics more vulnerable to developing alcoholism themselves, they also are often subjected to many adverse conditions associated with alcoholism—conditions ranging from economic hardship to physical abuse in some cases.''[7]

## ? ? ?
## HOW CAN THE FAMILY COPE WITH ALCOHOLISM?

Ideally, families should provide members with such basic necessities as food, clothes, and shelter. A family should also supply love, safety, security, and the opportunity to grow and become independent individuals. The parents should be role models from whom their children learn about love, caring, respect, and tolerance for individual differences, which make it possible for them to mature, leave home, and start families of their own.

But the family with an alcoholic member often falls far short of these goals. The family feels unstable, dispirited, broken apart, and insecure. With alcoholism, the home atmosphere is tense and uneasy, members show little love or trust, and physical or sexual abuse is a frequent danger.

Today experts are studying the factors at work in alcoholic families. They know that family and marital problems often start because of problem drinking. But they have also learned that spouses and children may contribute to the drinker's habit and make it worse. Some families allow heavy drinking to continue rather than deal with serious family problems, and keep the habit going in exchange for keeping the family together.

While alcoholism treatment programs help people with alcohol dependence to stop drinking and improve their life-styles, family and marital therapy and various self-help groups help families of alcoholics to improve their own well-being. They help the family face the truth about alcoholism, understand their own emotions, and speed up recovery.

But before discussing the full impact of these changes on the family, let's learn the facts about alcoholism and the individual drinker.

# 2
# THE
# ALCOHOLIC

Did you know?

○ Alcoholism affects about 10 percent of all adult Americans.[1]

○ At least 3 out of 100 deaths in the United States can be attributed to alcohol-related causes.[2]

○ Cirrhosis of the liver, caused by alcohol abuse, was the ninth leading cause of death in the United States.[3]

??? 

## WHAT IS ALCOHOL?

Alcohol is the most widely used and abused drug in the United States today. It is found in all beers and wines, and in whiskeys. The alcohol in all of these drinks is the same. Only the percentage of alcohol and the flavor of the drink differ. To a chemist, alcohol is ethyl alcohol or ethanol. Its chemical formula is $C_2H_5OH$.

Standard servings of whiskey, wine, and beer contain about the same amount of alcohol. A standard drink is either a "shot" of one and a half ounces of whiskey or other distilled spirit or liquor, a five-ounce glass of table wine, or a twelve-ounce can of beer. Each of these contains about half an ounce of ethyl alcohol.

Many people have false ideas about alcohol. For

example, many do not know that wine coolers, a very popular drink among young people, contain alcohol. According to a recent study, junior and senior high school students drink 35 percent of all wine coolers sold in the United States. But most of the students surveyed did not know that wine coolers are an alcoholic beverage. Misled by the advertising and packaging of these products, many teenagers do not realize that wine coolers often include more alcohol than a typical mixed drink.[4]

In the same way, some drinkers think that so-called "light" beers have a smaller alcohol content than regular beers. As a matter of fact, light beers may contain just as much alcohol as those that do not claim to be light.

In most states, the labels on beer and similar beverages do not disclose the drink's alcohol content. Although the alcohol content varies by brand and by state, consumers cannot tell by looking at the can or bottle how much alcohol they are consuming.

The 1990 "Dietary Guidelines for Americans," published by the United States Department of Agriculture and the Department of Health and Human Services, opposes the consumption of alcoholic beverages. Alcohol, they say, supplies calories, but few or no nutrients. According to the guidelines, "If adult men elect to drink alcoholic beverages, they should not drink more than two drinks per day; adult women should not drink more than one." Consuming greater quantities of alcohol than these levels is called "high-risk drinking."[5]

The United States Surgeon General also warns women not to drink alcoholic beverages during pregnancy because of the risk of birth defects and other health problems. In fact, the Surgeon General advises people using medicines (even those sold over-the-counter), those with a history of alcohol-related problems, and those at high risk for AIDS, to avoid alcohol completely.[6]

## WHO IS AN ALCOHOLIC?

Alcoholics are compulsive drinkers, that is, individuals who cannot keep their drinking under control. Frequently, alcoholics intend to have only one or two drinks but find it impossible to stop, and end up consuming eight or ten, or even twelve drinks at one sitting. Once they start, alcoholics will almost always drink themselves to drunkenness.

How can you separate social drinkers who occasionally abuse alcohol from alcoholics? Both groups drink because they like the way alcohol makes them feel. But when alcoholics drink, they usually lose control and drink to excess.

Most alcoholics set out to drink in the same way and in the same quantities as nonalcoholics. But they simply cannot. Their need and desire for liquor is so overpowering that it is beyond their control. Many experience it as a stronger drive than any other in their lives, no matter how much it makes them—and others—suffer.

Often people who drink too much realize that they have a drinking problem. They may have tried to overcome their dependency on alcohol and failed, leading some to give up hope and become even more alcohol-dependent.

Alcoholics resort to a number of reasons and excuses to explain and justify their drinking. They blame others. ("My boss is giving me a hard time." "My wife is always nagging." "All my friends go out drinking every night and I go along.")

They say they don't really "need" alcohol. ("I can quit any time I want to." "As soon as things get settled, I'll stop.")

The National Institute on Drugs and Alcohol (NIDAA) has prepared a checklist to judge if someone is an alcoholic. Here are some Yes/No questions adapted from

19

the NIDAA checklist. Answer them for a family member or friend—or even yourself.

Does the person

o drink frequently to escape from everyday stress and problems?

o drink more than most people?

o drink alone or sneak away and hide when drinking?

o show an increasing dependence on alcohol, drinking more and more?

o feel guilty about drinking and promise to drink less?

o think and talk only about drinking?

o gulp his or her drinks?

o blame others for the drinking problem?

o deny that there is a drinking problem?

o minimize the amount consumed?

o sometimes forget what happened during the drinking period?

o need a drink at a certain time?

o lose time from work or school due to drinking?

o lose control while drinking?

o seem irritable, defensive, jealous, moody, and easily angered after drinking?

o deny everything or get upset if anyone criticizes or complains about his or her drinking?

o have physical complaints—low energy, weight loss, sleeplessness—that may be related to drinking?

o feel worthless or depressed due to drinking behavior?

o avoid friends and social activities because of the drinking problem?

o make up excuses for continuing to drink?

One or more "Yes" answers, according to the NIDAA, may well indicate a problem with alcohol and someone on the way to becoming an alcoholic.

??? 

## ARE THERE TEENAGED ALCOHOLICS?

In 1991, a government report showed that 10.6 million of 20.7 million teenagers in grades seven through twelve have had alcoholic drinks—even though all fifty states have set twenty-one as the minimum legal drinking age. Eight million of the teenagers drink at least once a week; 450,000 drink at least five or more drinks at a sitting. If the average class of high school students has thirty students, that means as many as twelve may be starting to have a problem with alcohol![7] Besides being illegal, drinking by minors has other dangers related to growth and development, particularly as it affects their immune, endocrine, and reproductive systems.

It is unlikely that all 8 million in the study who drink weekly will become alcoholics. Yet, if the drinking patterns they are establishing as teenagers continue into adulthood, alcohol will become an increasing threat to their own health, as well as to the well-being of the people around them.

The age at which youngsters start drinking has been going down over the last several decades. "The age of first alcohol use in the 1930s was seventeen for boys and nineteen for women," says Dr. Margaret Bean-Bayog, a psychiatrist in Newton, Massachusetts. "Now it's much more common for a thirteen-year-old to have had a drink."[8] And some surveys have found that kids as young as ten or twelve are already drinking—and are urging their friends and classmates to do the same.

Generally, experts find that the young drinkers who

started drinking at an early age need the most help. It is difficult, however, to predict the outcome of adolescent drinking. Some children who experiment with liquor in their early teens have stopped drinking by high school. Most, though, have not.

As shown by the results of the recent national survey "Youth and Alcohol," "binge" drinking (drinking five or more drinks in a row) is on an alarming upward trend. More than 5 million students have binged—3 million within the month before the survey. And 454,000 binge at least once a week.[9]

Unfortunately, many students lack essential knowledge about alcohol and its effects. Nationwide, about 20 million students do not understand how and why alcohol causes intoxication; nearly 6 million are unsure of the legal age to purchase alcohol; almost 3 million are not aware that a person can die from drinking alcohol; most do not know the relative alcoholic contents of different drinks.

? ? ?

## HOW DOES ALCOHOL AFFECT WOMEN AND THE ELDERLY?

Because statistics show that most alcoholics are men, women alcoholics have only recently come to the attention of the experts. Among the new findings of the federal government: women who are unmarried, but living with a partner, have the highest rates of drinking problems; women in their twenties and early thirties are at the highest risk for alcoholism; women with heavy-drinking husbands or live-in partners make up another high-risk group.

As for the elderly, the government estimates that 10 percent of those over sixty are dependent on alcohol. While alcohol consumption patterns are lower in the elderly than in younger age groups, alcohol abuse is one of the five most frequent diagnoses for Medicare (over age sixty-five) patients admitted to hospitals.[10]

Overall alcohol consumption remains the same or goes down in the later years. A number of reasons have been given: growing health problems, increased sensitivity to the effects of alcohol, a fear of harmful interactions between alcohol and medicines, decreased income, and changes in life-style associated with retirement.

Even though alcohol consumption generally drops in the elderly, heavy drinking may also begin around this time. Individuals who find retirement difficult to handle and have a history of avoiding personal problems are at risk for alcoholism. Day after day without going to work and without structure may make the elderly man or woman feel at loose ends, depressed, and fearful.

Old age may bring pressures and losses that turn some older people to alcohol for relief. The struggle to make ends meet, the illness or recent death of a spouse, the loneliness, boredom, and emotional stress of aging make some especially vulnerable to excessive drinking. Housing problems, falls or accidents, poor nutrition, inadequate self-care, lack of physical exercise, and social isolation are other factors that may contribute to a drinking habit that starts late in life.

An important deciding factor in so-called late-onset drinking seems to be how the person used alcohol throughout his or her life. Moderate drinkers who saw alcohol as an emotional outlet or relief from boredom are more at risk for alcoholism as they grow older. Those who were merely social drinkers and who never saw alcohol as an emotional release are at lower risk.

The over-sixty-five group is especially vulnerable to the addictive effects of alcohol, as well as to physical damage and depression. This may be because the older person's body systems do not function as well as they do in younger individuals.

The liver, which breaks down the alcohol in the body, still does its job in the elderly, but it doesn't do it as quickly or as efficiently. Therefore, the effects of alcohol are stronger and more long-lasting. The cardiovascular system is also more greatly affected. In fact, older drinkers with a tendency to high blood pressure are at risk for blackout, memory loss, and in severe cases, stroke.

Drinking alcohol can also cause dehydration for the elderly. The result may be kidney damage, lethargy, and loss of appetite. The condition may result in stomach irritation and, if drinking persists, ulcers and stomach bleeding.

But the most severe effects of alcohol abuse on the elderly are in the brain. When subjected to alcohol, the brain of a seventy-year old has more severe memory lapses than the brains of younger individuals. Habitual older drinkers often forget to eat, forget to lock the house, and forget whether or not they took their medication. The memory lapses make car crashes and accidents around the house more likely to happen.

Seniors find that alcohol affects already disturbed sleeping patterns and increases fatigue. Sleeping at night becomes even more difficult; many drinks produce a very deep sleep that leaves the elderly person feeling groggy and tired upon awakening.

Alcohol can also lead to psychological depression and make depression worse when it already exists. Doctors find that depression among the elderly is more complicated and difficult to treat if alcohol is a factor.

The effects of alcohol on an older person are often made worse due to the presence of other drugs in the body. Most elderly persons take medicines for physical problems and these often interact with alcohol. In some cases, the drug and alcohol make each other stronger, so that the right dose becomes an overdose. In other cases, alcohol may cause the drug to lose its effect.

### ? ? ?
## WHAT ABOUT ALCOHOLISM AMONG THE HOMELESS AND MINORITIES?

Lifetime alcohol abuse among the homeless ranges as high as 63 percent, with the greatest risk in the middle-aged group.[11] In this population, heavy drinking seems to be a way of coping with the physical and emotional stresses associated with being homeless. The exact opposite, though, may be just as true: alcoholism itself may increase the danger that the individual will become homeless and stay on the streets.

Generally speaking, the homeless population suffers all kinds of health problems—problems that are only increased by alcohol abuse and dependence. To take just one example, male alcohol abusers are almost twice as likely as nonabusers to have high blood pressure.[12]

Alcohol abuse accompanied by drug abuse and mental illness among the homeless is especially significant. In a recent study, more than one-fourth of homeless alcoholics abused other drugs in addition to alcohol and more than half of female abusers and one-fourth of male abusers were mentally ill. One Los Angeles researcher found that 69 percent of those with lifetime alcohol abuse had psychiatric difficulties.[13]

These findings are important for setting public policy for the homeless. They suggest that the homeless with alcohol and/or psychiatric problems need to have health and mental health care, along with housing and job opportunities. The loss or lack of a job may not be the primary reason for being homeless. Instead, a lack of money and a family crisis, complicated by alcohol problems, may be the main cause of the homeless condition.

The four largest racial and ethnic minority groups in

25

the United States are blacks (12 percent of the population), Hispanics (9 percent), Asian-Americans (approximately 3 percent), and American Indians and Alaska Natives (less than 1 percent).[14]

Although blacks have low rates of heavy drinking, they are at extremely high risk for health problems in which alcohol is a factor. Hispanics have high rates of heavy drinking and a higher prevalence of drinking-related problems than other groups. Asian-Americans have the lowest rates of heavy drinking and the lowest levels of drinking related problems. And American Indian and Alaska Native groups as a whole have high mortality rates that are likely to be alcohol caused.[15]

# 3
# EFFECTS
## ON THE BODY
## AND MIND

Did you know?

- Problem drinking shortens an alcoholic's life an average of twelve years for men and fifteen years for women.[1]

- One out of three suicides occur after drinking.[2]

- Alcohol use by pregnant women is the leading known cause of mental retardation in newborns.[3]

? ? ?

## HOW DOES ALCOHOL
## AFFECT THE BODY?

Alcohol affects every organ system in the body either directly or indirectly. The effects, though, are not the same for everyone. Some people, for genetic or other reasons, have a much stronger reaction to alcohol than others. As we said, Asian-Americans have few drinking-related problems. Experts believe it is partly because of the nausea and flushing that many Asians experience when they drink alcohol.

The body's reaction to alcohol also depends on how much the person drinks, over how long a period, and whether the drinking is done in short spurts or whether it is continuous.

The liver is the main organ responsible for breaking down, or metabolizing, alcohol in the body. It is not surprising then that the liver is severely affected by heavy alcohol use.

Almost all very heavy drinkers suffer from a liver disease, known as fatty liver, in which fat cells accumulate in the liver. About 10 to 35 percent of alcoholics have an even more serious liver condition, called alcoholic hepatitis, which causes an inflammation of liver tissue and death of liver cells.[4] Both fatty liver and alcoholic hepatitis are conditions that usually clear up once the alcoholic stops drinking.

Of all alcohol-caused liver diseases, the most dangerous is cirrhosis, which causes permanent damage to liver cells. Estimates of the percentage of drinkers with cirrhosis vary from 10 to 20 percent. Although the number of deaths from cirrhosis have been declining in the United States, it still ranks high as a cause of death.[5]

For many years, doctors believed that poor nutrition combined with alcohol caused cirrhosis in alcoholics. Many habitual drinkers do not eat properly; more than 10 percent of the calories they require may come from alcohol. (Although alcohol contains calories, it does not contain the vitamins and minerals necessary for good health.) Doctors thought that the lack of these nutrients might cause the cirrhosis. Today, however, experts hold that alcoholism may be the direct cause of the cirrhosis, while malnutrition is a contributing cause.

Heavy alcohol use can also result in significant damage to the digestive system. It can cause inflammation of the esophagus, make any ulcers worse, and lead to increased cases of inflammation or cancer of the stomach. Alcohol increases the flow of digestive secretions, injures the stomach lining, and slows down the emptying of the stomach. And, more than any other substance, alcohol causes both acute and chronic inflammation of the pancreas, a condition known as pancreatitis.

Chronic alcohol abuse can also cause damage to the heart muscles responsible for pumping blood throughout the body. Patients who stop drinking, though, have a rather good chance of restoring the function of those muscles. Alcohol can also cause problems with the normal pumping action of the heart, making it pump much faster or even start to quiver and shake.

High alcohol consumption appears, too, to influence a person's blood pressure. Blood pressure rises in individuals who have about three drinks a day; blood pressure reaches dangerously high levels in individuals having six or more drinks a day. Scientists estimate that alcohol abuse causes between 5 and 24 percent of all cases of high blood pressure.[6]

The increased pressure may cause an accident in a weakened blood vessel in the brain, resulting in a stroke. Damage to the arteries that bring blood to the heart is known as coronary heart disease.

Alcohol does not seem to have any effect on breast and lung cancer, two of the most common forms of the disease. There does, however, seem to be a link between alcohol abuse and cancer of the liver, esophagus, and larynx, and of the prostate gland in men.

? ? ?

## HOW DOES ALCOHOL AFFECT THE MIND?

Alcohol is one of the few substances that can cross into human brain cells. Generally speaking, alcohol tends to weaken the part of the brain that controls behavior. A small quantity of alcohol helps people feel good. They feel more relaxed, less inhibited and shy, and enjoy pleasurable sensations.

Greater amounts of alcohol, say two and a half drinks within an hour, start to affect the drinker's judgment. Some drinkers become loud and silly; others pick fights and become abusive. Their self-control decreases, so that they do things they would not do when not drinking. People who would not think of breaking the law when sober, commit crimes with alcohol in their systems. A person who normally would not take chances, might drive a car recklessly at almost twice the speed limit.

Consuming five drinks within an hour brings the level of alcohol in the blood to 0.10 percent, the point at which a person is considered legally drunk. The parts of the brain involved with muscle coordination do not function well. Speech is slurred. Control over the limbs is limited and it becomes almost impossible to make fine, careful hand and finger movements. Reaction time is much slower.

When ten alcoholic drinks are consumed in an hour, the blood-alcohol level goes up to 0.20 percent. Now, even more of the brain is affected. The emotions swing wildly; anger, love, hatred, laughter follow one another without pause and without cause. Judgment, coordination, and perception are limited and unreliable. Some people even pass out and become unconscious.

Twelve or more drinks within an hour may paralyze the part of the brain that controls breathing. In these cases, the person goes into a coma and can die.

Many of the effects of a drinking binge, in which someone has anywhere from two to ten drinks in an hour, disappear in time. But long-term, heavy alcohol abuse has more lasting effects on the brain. Research studies show that between 50 and 75 percent of alcoholics experience difficulties in learning, remembering, perceiving, and solving problems.[7]

Some chronic, heavy drinkers have permanent damage leading to problems in brain function. Dementia, or general mental impairment, is one such condition. Nearly 20 percent of all patients admitted to state hospitals with dementia are found to be alcohol abusers.[8]

Other brain-related symptoms of heavy drinking are blackouts, seizures, and hallucinations. The famous pink elephants that drunks report seeing are an example of an hallucination.

### ? ? ?
## WHY DO SOME PEOPLE DRINK TOO MUCH?

The reason many alcoholics drink until they are drunk has long puzzled researchers. New findings say that a key factor may be the structure of the alcoholic's brain. The brains of alcoholics differ organically from those of non-alcoholics.

For individual drinkers whose brains are different, an imbalance in the chemicals found in the brain may cause them to drink until they are intoxicated. In these cases, loss of control is not related to personality, character, or lack of willpower, but rather to a malfunction of the brain.

Researchers are now seeking the genetic component that regulates the chemicals in the brain—chemicals that, when out of balance, make it impossible for alcoholics to drink moderately or reasonably. What researchers have learned so far leads them to believe that some individuals may be predisposed to alcoholism. Once alcohol reaches their brains, it causes chemical changes which result in uncontrolled drinking.

### ? ? ?
## WHEN IS THE ALCOHOLIC AT RISK FOR SUICIDE?

Alcoholics are at risk for suicide after lengthy spells of drinking that cause depression and intense feelings of guilt—emotions that often precede suicide attempts. This may occur when the problem drinker "hits bottom" after a long drinking bout, or during a relapse after having been sober for some time.

Alcoholics may also attempt to put an end to their lives when they stop drinking after years of heavy alcohol consumption. Feelings of powerlessness may overwhelm the alcoholic, as well as an awareness, perhaps for the first time, of all that he or she has lost as a result of the alcoholism.

Individuals at greatest risk, however, are those who have made a previous suicide attempt, have a history of mental illness, have a relative who committed suicide, and/or are faced with recent losses such as the death of a loved one (especially to suicide), the loss of a job, or divorce.

The alcoholic is at particularly high risk during times of crisis. And because of his drinking habit, the alcoholic usually experiences frequent crises and losses. Studies have shown that most alcoholics who have killed themselves have lost someone close to them within the six-week period before the suicide.[9]

Alcoholics, we know, use their drinking to feel better—to escape, to numb their hurt, to fill a sense of emptiness. Since alcohol is a depressant, however, the good feelings last only a short while, leaving the alcoholic feeling even more depressed and guilty. This leads to a vicious cycle: depression to drinking, alcohol to more depression, depression to more drinking, and so on.

The warning signs of suicide include a sudden change in behavior, personality, sleep, or eating patterns; loss of interest in school; inability to hold a job; withdrawal from family and friends; impulsive actions and inappropriate risk-taking; mood swings; and greater than usual feelings of anger or anxiety. The immediate danger signals include talking about or hinting at suicide and an obsession with death.

Professionals who work with suicidal alcoholics offer them hope. They try to get them to talk about their feelings, no matter how scary or painful, to bring down their level of anxiety and to make them feel truly understood. But even experts, when suicide is involved, frequently get family members and friends involved in the helping process.

## WHAT IS TOLERANCE AND DEPENDENCY?

People who start drinking heavily and regularly over a period of time find that they need to drink more and more to get the same high, the same intoxicated feeling. This significant change is known as tolerance. It is as though their bodies have gotten used to the alcohol and they need to drink ever greater quantities to feel the same effect. The body has become tolerant of the alcohol and requires additional amounts to achieve what smaller amounts achieved before.

Scientists are slowly unlocking the secrets of tolerance and why and how it develops. So far they have found that it is a highly complex process that involves the nervous system and the way messages travel between the nerve cells in the brain.

At the same time as drinkers are developing their tolerance for alcohol, they are also increasing their craving for alcohol. Experts call this dependency. More and more, the alcoholics depend on getting a drink as often as they crave it.

Traditionally, the powerful craving, or need, to obtain more and more alcohol is called an addiction. People who become addicted to alcohol have two kinds of dependency—physical and psychological.

Physical dependence occurs when people have become so used to a drug that they need it to function

33

without pain. For drinkers who are physically dependent, "normal" now means they have alcohol in their body. If they don't have alcohol in their bloodstream, they feel sick; they only feel "well" when they are drinking. Users not only *want* the drink—they *must have* it! Without a steady, reliable source of alcohol, they suffer great distress and discomfort.

Psychological dependence sets in when users believe that a drug is an important and necessary part of life and that life will not be as good without it. Even when their bodies do not demand the drug, their minds signal a need for alcohol.

Instead of addiction, the term "psychoactive substance dependence" is often used today. The diagnosis of "psychoactive substance dependence" is made if at least three of the following statements are true:

*The substance is taken in larger amounts or over a longer period than the person intended.*

*There is a persistent desire, or unsuccessful efforts to stop.*

*The person spends a great deal of time trying to get the substance, taking it, or recovering from its effects.*

*Using the substance disrupts important social obligations or work activities.*

*The person continues to use the substance despite knowing that it is causing problems (for example, drinking even though it makes an ulcer worse).*

*There is a marked tolerance; the person needs increased amounts of the substance to become intoxicated or feels less of an effect if using the same amount.*

34

*There are withdrawal symptoms (see below).*

*The substance is taken to avoid the withdrawal symptoms.*[10]

### ? ? ?
### WHAT IS WITHDRAWAL?

Withdrawal is a term for a number of physical and psychological symptoms that sometimes occur in people who are alcohol dependent and find themselves deprived of liquor when they want some. The symptoms may show up in alcoholics who finish a bottle and find themselves unable to get another, in those undergoing treatment or in jail and completely removed from any source of alcohol, or in persons who are trying to stop drinking on their own.

The mildest symptoms of withdrawal are known as "rebound effects." Most of these symptoms originate in the central nervous system. Among the common symptoms are tremors and shakes, sweating, nausea, cramps, what people call a "hangover" headache, and heightened nervousness and jumpiness. These withdrawal reactions may occur when a heavy drinker merely has less than usual or when a moderate drinker has no alcohol at all. The duration of the withdrawal symptoms and their severity depends largely on how much the person had been drinking and for how long. In some cases, the signs of withdrawal can appear as quickly as overnight. The alcoholic wakes up with trembling hands and a desperate need to have a drink—even before breakfast!

Longtime, heavy drinkers usually suffer more serious symptoms when they stop drinking. Some have hallucinations—they hear threatening voices that sound real and frightening. Convulsive seizures sometimes go along with severe alcohol withdrawal. The eyes roll back in the head, the body muscles contract, and the person loses consciousness. The alcoholic may remain in this state for up to eight hours.

### ? ? ?
## WHAT IS A BLACKOUT?

Drinkers may experience a blackout after they have been drinking steadily and heavily. Although the drinkers remain conscious and awake, they suffer a loss of memory and cannot remember what happened during the drinking period. Blackouts explain why many alcoholics hurt those around them and then later seem not to care—they may simply not remember what they did. Blackouts are not a common reaction to normal social drinking and almost always indicate a person has a serious problem with alcohol.

"Passing out" is entirely different. Passing out usually means the drinkers have lost consciousness because their bodies cannot tolerate the amount of alcohol they have consumed. Alcohol is a depressant; it dampens, limits, and slows down the functioning of the brain. As more and more alcohol is consumed, increasingly large areas of the brain are shut down.

While passing out usually indicates simply that the drinker has consumed too much alcohol, it can, however, be life threatening. The loss of consciousness becomes critical when it is a result of combining alcohol with other drugs or of consuming too much alcohol in too short a time.

### ? ? ?
## WHAT ARE DTS?

Delirium tremens (DTs) is the most serious of all withdrawal reactions. Delirium refers to especially terrifying hallucinations and mental confusion. The person may see imaginary bugs on the walls, feel insects crawling over the body, and be totally confused about time and place.

Tremens refers to the uncontrollable shaking, agitation, fast pulse, and high fever that are part of this condition.

Delirium tremens may start anytime between two and seven days after the last drink. About 30 percent of all alcoholics who have seizures later experience delirium tremens. Since DTs can be the beginning of a dangerous medical crisis, it is important that family members be alert to the possibility of serious withdrawal symptoms. There are medications that help to alleviate or prevent many of the more serious withdrawal reactions.

Delirium tremens is the most severe form of alcoholic withdrawal. One out of every five people who goes into DTs dies. Most of the others pass through the worst of the symptoms in a few days, fall into a deep sleep, and awake with little memory of what happened.

### ❓ ❓ ❓
## WHAT IS FETAL
## ALCOHOL SYNDROME?

In 1973 a new name entered the medical vocabulary—fetal alcohol syndrome, or FAS. It was coined by doctors to describe the cluster of physical and psychological conditions found in babies born to alcoholic mothers. While fetal alcohol syndrome is most common among poor people, it occurs in middle-class homes as well.

Experts now find that FAS is one of the top three known causes of birth defects. Fetal alcohol syndrome is also the third largest cause of birth-related mental retardation.[11] About 5,000 babies are born each year with full-blown FAS; another 35,000 infants suffer from less severe damage caused by their mothers' drinking, according to the National Council on Alcoholism and Drug Dependence.[12]

Babies with FAS differ from normal babies in several ways. They are short and underweight and fall within the lowest 10 percent for length and weight. They often show malformations of the brain and skull and have characteristic facial features, including small eye openings, a thin upper lip, a long, flat face, and a long groove in the middle of the upper lip.

The greatest damage, though, occurs to the central nervous system of FAS babies. As a result, these infants have difficulties in learning, attention, memory, and problem solving. Many are mentally retarded and endure these mental deficits for the rest of their lives.

The central nervous system damage also leads to problems in behavior. Babies with FAS are hyperactive, unable to sit or stand still for very long. They act impulsively, are poorly coordinated, and often have impaired speech and hearing.

Michael Dorris is a Dartmouth University professor and author who adopted three children with birth defects caused by parental alcohol abuse. Despite his best efforts, these children have been arrested for shoplifting, sexual misconduct, and violent behavior. "They maintain no enduring friendships, set for themselves no realistic goals, can call upon no bedrock inner values to distinguish right from wrong, safe from dangerous," he said.[13]

In general, the more severe the mother's drinking problem during pregnancy, the more severe the symptoms of the FAS in the infant. Even moderate alcohol consumption during pregnancy can cause some symptoms. Thus far researchers have not found a safe level of alcohol intake, one that has no effect at all on the baby. For that reason, most doctors recommend that mothers have absolutely no alcohol while they are pregnant.

??? 

## DO ALCOHOLICS HAVE SIMILAR PERSONALITY TRAITS?

Alcoholics can be of any age, background, income level, social, or ethnic group. Yet they all share certain similar personality traits. Alcoholics tend to be hyperactive, have a short attention span, are unable to deal with frustration or pain, and have trouble coping with difficult situations. Alcoholics have also been described as unstable, unpredictable, and impulsive.

Often, alcoholics are people who seek immediate gratification of their needs—they look for the "easy way" to solve their problems. At first, alcohol strikes some people as the perfect solution. It relieves distress, gives pleasure, and builds self-esteem. Also, it generally alters reality so that problems become less demanding and conflicts seem easier to control.

Alcohol abuse may also be a learned response to problem solving. Alcoholism is established by the continual practice of turning to alcohol to remove discomfort, relieve pressure, and ease tension. After some time with this regime, drinking may become the preferred way to handle a problem.

Of course, the reverse may also be true. Dr. George Vaillant, who directed a research study of 600 men, found that psychological instability does not cause alcoholism. "Alcoholism causes the stress," he writes. "It puts people out of control of their lives. It makes everything harder."[14]

Among the most common reasons alcohol abusers give for drinking are escape, loneliness, poor emotional control, and fear.

Drinking may be used as a way of avoiding unpleasant problems, instead of facing them. Fred, a carpenter, says, "My boss kept on picking on me. 'That's no good!' 'Can't you move any faster?' 'What's the matter, are you stupid?' So I began taking a big, stiff shot of whiskey every day just before going to work. Then I added a few more drinks during lunch. It was the only way I could get through the day."

Drinking may be used to lessen the pain of not being able to make friends or being separated from family because of distance or death. Sixty-five-year-old Gerald commented, "Within a couple of months, my wife died, my daughter moved to France, and two of my good friends retired to Florida. The evenings with nothing to do were the most painful. At first, I began having a cocktail before dinner, which helped me to relax and made the time pass faster. Then I had two drinks, three drinks, and before I knew it, I was drinking all afternoon. Sometimes I got so drunk that I fell asleep and didn't wake until the next morning."

Many use drinking to help ease emotional problems and difficult interpersonal relationships. Jack says, "Anita and I were engaged. We had even picked the date for the wedding. Then she met this guy and, like, two weeks later, she tells me our engagement is off and she's going to marry this new guy. The news hit me like a ton of bricks, so I went out and got roaring drunk. But I never could get over what she did to me. So, the next day I got drunk again, and the following day, too. Now I'm drunk almost every day—and it's all Anita's fault!"

Often drinking gives shy, frightened, or threatened people a false sense of self-confidence. Kevin is an insurance agent who calls on his customers. "Every day I go to people's houses and try to talk them into buying insurance from me. It's always been hard for me to talk to strangers, so I got into the habit of keeping a bottle of whiskey in my car. That way, I could have a quick shot if I was nervous about meeting someone. By now, though, I have a drink before meeting each client. Sometimes I go through a whole bottle of whiskey in one day."

Despite the similarities, alcohol-dependent persons are also a diverse group with many different personality traits, life experiences, family characteristics, and social status. Knowing these differences plays a big part in determining why alcohol dependence arises in some individuals and not in others.

# 4

# CAUSES OF
# ALCOHOLISM

Did you know?

○ Sons of alcoholic fathers are four times as likely to become alcoholic as the sons of nonalcoholics.[1]

○ Daughters of alcoholic mothers are three times as likely to become alcoholic as the daughters of nonalcoholics.[2]

○ One-third of alcoholics have one or more parents who are also alcoholic.[3]

? ? ?

## DOES ALCOHOLISM
## RUN IN FAMILIES?

Research evidence shows the greatest risk factor for alcoholism is genetic. Women are just as likely to inherit a susceptibility to alcoholism as are men. The sons, daughters, brothers, and sisters of alcoholics are more likely than others to become alcoholics. Some people call alcoholism the "three generation" disease. That is, it seems to be passed from parents to children and from them to the children's children.

Two well-known and important studies in Scandinavian countries involving twins separated soon after birth, and reared by separate parents, point to a genetic factor. One study compared sets of twins, some identical (with the same genes) and some fraternal (born at the same time, but with different genes). In cases where one identical twin was an alcoholic, the other twin was apt to be as well. Among fraternal twins, however, far fewer alcoholic pairs were found.

The other study looked at a number of children who were adopted before they were six weeks old. More children whose biological parents were alcoholics grew up to have drinking problems than did children of nondrinking parents—no matter the drinking habits of the adoptive parents. In other words, children born to an alcoholic parent, despite how or where they were raised, were more likely to become alcoholics.

A 1992 study on alcoholism as a genetic disorder, however, presents some startling results. According to a report by Matt McGue, a psychologist at the University of Minnesota, research on 356 patients in treatment for alcoholism and their twins found that environmental factors are far stronger than heredity in female alcoholics, and in male alcoholics who develop drinking problems in adulthood. The strong genetic influence showed up only in men who developed drinking problems before the age of twenty.[4]

Although most authorities still believe that alcoholism runs in families, they are not sure why. While some forms of alcohol dependence are almost surely inherited, others seem less likely to be so, and still others seem to have no obvious genetic connection. Genetic predisposition, however, does not mean predestination, and researchers are now studying factors associated with resistance to alcoholism.

? ? ?

## IS ALCOHOLISM A DISEASE?

The view of alcoholism as a lifelong, chronic illness was presented best by Dr. E.M. Jellinek in 1946. Dr. Jellinek's theory holds that the more a person drinks, the more he or she needs to drink. A person's move toward alcoholism begins with the first drink. The disease progresses from moderate drinking to heavier consumption and has little to do with choice or willpower.

The condition continues until the alcoholic suffers a complete breakdown or stops drinking. To stop drinking, though, is to arrest the disease, not cure it. If drinking starts again, the cycle will repeat itself.

Today, alcohol dependence is considered a disease in which a genetic predisposition is affected by environmental factors. Experts say that alcoholism fits the pattern of most major chronic diseases. For example, high blood pressure is genetically linked, yet such environmental factors as salt intake and smoking may play important roles in how the disease develops.

Alcohol dependence is not an infectious disease like measles, or a disease like cancer, in which cells multiply wildly. Rather, in alcohol dependence, body and mind interact in complex ways.

To be considered a disease, a condition must have a certain set of symptoms and follow a certain course and outcome. Alcohol-dependent persons experience such symptoms as an intense craving to drink, severe physical effects from drinking, and withdrawal when drinking stops. In time, they develop a tolerance to alcohol, and need increased quantities to get the same effect.

Studies of thousands of alcoholics show that most pass through four separate phases. Take the typical case of Dan, who was married, with a young daughter, and worked as a lawyer in a large Chicago law firm.

Dan started drinking while he was in college, but only in social situations. He wanted to feel part of the group and liked the calm, relaxed feeling that alcohol gave him. Once he started working, he found that his job had a lot of pressure and required very long hours. Sometimes he didn't get home until nine or ten o'clock at night. On these nights he had a few drinks before dinner. Then he would insist on a nightcap before going to bed. "I need the liquor to help me unwind," he told his wife.

After about two years on the job, Dan entered phase two. He kept a bottle of whiskey hidden in an office desk drawer. Three, four, five times a day, when no one was watching, he would take a big gulp of whiskey. Sometimes he drank so much that he had trouble doing his work. At these times, Dan was embarrassed and vowed to stop drinking forever as soon as he finished the bottle in his desk. Nevertheless, he always broke his promises.

Then Dan began to show signs that he was in the third phase. Even though he denied it, he lost all control around alcohol. Once started, he could not stop. With each drink, he thought, "Just one more drink and everything will be all right." But things did not improve. Several times the senior lawyer in his firm found fault in the work Dan was doing. And his wife and daughter found it more and more difficult to get along with him at home.

Soon Dan was in the fourth and final phase. Everyone knew he had become an alcoholic. The senior lawyer forced him to take a leave of absence from his job. His wife and daughter moved out and went to live with his wife's parents. Dan spent most of his time at home, usually drinking until he passed out.

The alcohol consumption took a toll on Dan's body and his mind. His voice became hoarse and low in pitch. His skin was pale and sallow. He lost weight, but his abdomen stuck way out. He perspired a great deal and had red palms and swollen ankles. His walk was unsteady, his movements awkward and uncoordinated. And most obvious of all, his nose grew red and swollen.

Along with a distorted sense of reality, Dan had

lapses of memory and was unable to learn anything new. His behavior was inconsistent; at times he would act normally, but then he would do something strange and unpredictable. He alternated periods of violence and aggression with times of depression and fearfulness.

Dan's story does not have a happy ending. Late one evening he got into his car, drove into traffic, and was hit by another car. An ambulance took Dan to the hospital, but he died the following day.

The question of whether alcoholism is an inherited disease, a symptom of an underlying condition, or an illness one acquires by choice has been argued and studied extensively. Most researchers now believe that alcoholism is a disease, and like other diseases, it does not have a single cause. Basically, everyone agrees on the following points:

*All alcoholics display clear symptoms that vary only slightly from one individual to another.*

*Alcoholism is a progressive condition that only worsens with time and, if left untreated, can be fatal.*

*The condition is due to a combination of genetic, psychological, and social factors—an interaction between the person, the substance, and the environment.*

? ? ?

## HOW DO PSYCHOLOGICAL FACTORS AFFECT DRINKING BEHAVIOR?

A high level of abnormal personality development and criminality is found in many families of alcoholics. Thus, poor mental health seems to be associated with the onset or development of certain forms of alcoholism.

As a child, this psychological theory holds, the alcoholic may have been rejected or abused by his or her parents. Young men who are jealous of their fathers may drink to bolster their self-image. Or they may drink because they were unsuccessful in school or in making friends. In studying the personality differences among young alcoholics and normal adolescents, psychologists find strong evidence that drinking is an attempt by some teenagers to overcome their feelings of inadequacy.

Some family members may be led to alcohol abuse by poor adult role models, according to this theory. The children learn to abuse alcohol from their parents, who also abuse alcohol. "Most drinking begins at the liquor cabinet at home," experts say. By age twelve, many youngsters probably know a significant number of people—in the family and out—who drink. Young people who see lots of alcohol consumed around them, as well as those whose parents abuse alcohol, are at high risk.

What about the drinkers who come from homes with nonalcoholic parents and are not surrounded by alcohol abuse? In fact, many teens who are problem drinkers have parents who are strongly opposed to their drinking. In these cases the heavy drinking may represent defiance of parental authority. Some young people start to drink as part of their rebellion. They may feel that they're not being allowed to grow up as fast as they would like. They know their parents are against alcohol, so by drinking they are striking back at their folks—and at society.

??? 

## IS SOME BIOCHEMICAL
## AGENT TO BLAME?

Many people drink, yet not everyone becomes addicted to alcohol. Some individuals have almost no reaction to alcohol, while others are easily intoxicated. Animal experiments, too, show that some can tolerate alcohol, while others cannot.

Individual susceptibility to alcoholism may be due to some biochemical imbalance in the system. Recent studies point to possible deficiencies of a chemical in the brain, the neurotransmitter serotonin. Rats that show a preference for alcohol have a lower level of serotonin in their brain. Experiments with serotonin levels and alcohol consumption show that as drinking goes up, the serotonin level drops.

Scientists are also finding that alcoholics and nonalcoholics may have differences in the activity of certain enzymes. The lowered activity of these enzymes could affect certain significant functions in the brain and could be a contributing factor that might lead to alcoholism. But it is also possible that a lower level of the enzymes is simply a result of heavy drinking.

Various groups of individuals show different responses to alcohol. The low incidence of alcoholism among Asians, for example, is sometimes ascribed to social factors. But several studies attribute the low incidence to the unpleasant reactions, such as flushing and nausea, that many Asians get to even small amounts of alcohol. No one is sure of the reason for this, but most researchers suspect that a change in one of the enzymes needed for the metabolism of alcohol causes the ill effects. Likewise, a high percentage of Jews have unpleasant reactions to modest amounts of alcohol. Biochemical agents, too, may account for the low incidence of alcoholism among Jewish people.

While recent research emphasizes genetic and biological risk factors that make some people more likely to become alcoholics once they start drinking, experts in several countries are trying to discover the exact genetic-biological elements involved.

## DO SOCIAL AND/OR CULTURAL FACTORS INFLUENCE THE RATE OF ALCOHOLISM?

Of course, alcoholism is not limited to any one group. Ethnic and religious affiliations, occupation, and social class all influence who drinks and how much.

By itself, freedom to drink does not always lead to alcoholism. Moderate drinking, proponents of this view say, is accepted in the Jewish, Chinese, and Italian cultures. Yet, all three show low rates of alcoholism. Russia, France, and Ireland, on the other hand, are nations where alcoholism is much more of an issue. Certain cultures have a higher rate of alcoholism because they accept the use of alcohol as a means of solving problems.

The differences, then, may come down to *why* people drink, not how much. Those who use alcohol for relief and escape seem to produce the highest rates of addiction.

The first drinks taken by adolescents are usually beer and wine. Ads usually try to give the message that drinking is a great way to make friends and have fun. The beautiful, well-tanned crowd on the beach with cans of beer in their hands look very happy. "What's wrong with that?" the ad seems to say. Experts estimate that a teenager watching an average amount of television sees as many as 2,500 alcohol advertisements a year![5]

Students bound for college tend to drink less than those who are not. But, by the age of nineteen or twenty, the college group is drinking just as much as their noncollege peers. Further, those in college "binge," that is, have at least five drinks on a single occasion, more often. The frequency of binge drinking among college-age drinkers has become a major cause for concern.

A society's beliefs concerning the causes of alcoholism determine how it handles the problem of heavy drinking. Where alcohol consumption is considered a crime, states or cities pass laws prohibiting drinking alcohol. Punishments can be as slight as a fine of a few dollars or as much as three years in jail.

In 1962, the United States Supreme Court ruled in the case of *Robinson v. California* that an illness cannot be considered a crime. Treating alcoholism as a disease, not a criminal act, means that the alcoholic cannot be punished for drinking or being drunk. The trend today is toward treatment and away from punishment.

Research into the causes of alcoholism continues. In an effort to explain the development of alcoholism, researchers are concentrating their efforts in three main areas: the physiological (the body itself), the psychological (the mind), and the social or cultural (society).

Physiological studies include research into genetic causes, physical factors in the body, abnormalities of the brain, and allergic reactions, any one of which might predispose an individual to develop alcoholism.

Psychological researchers are mostly exploring how individuals use alcohol as a tension reducer or as an escape from emotional stress.

Social and cultural researchers are looking at the social setting in which one learns to drink and the cultural attitudes surrounding the use of alcohol.

# 5
# CHILDREN OF
# ALCOHOLICS

Did you know?

○ There are an estimated 30 million children of alcoholics—one in eight of all Americans—in the United States.[1]

○ About 7 million children of alcoholics are under the age of eighteen and live at home.[2]

○ Over 60 percent of all teenagers who attempt suicide come from alcoholic families.[3]

??? 

## WHO ARE THE CHILDREN OF ALCOHOLICS?

Children of alcoholics (COAs) are young people—rich and poor, black, white, and Hispanic, living in cities, suburbs, and rural areas, and from every part of the country—who live in homes where a parent or other family member drinks habitually and to excess. Most often, the drinking problem causes these children considerable pain and difficulty in their day-to-day lives.

Although the way genetic factors interact with environmental influences varies from individual to individual, certain common symptoms are found among COAs. Generally, these include low self-esteem; an unusually high preoccupation with the needs, feelings, and judgments of others; guilt for causing the bad situation; loneliness; a sense of helplessness over the family's troubles; fears of abandonment; distrust of self and others; and chronic depression.

For most COAs, home is not a warm, loving, and secure place where they can grow and develop into independent, mature adults. Instead, home is a hostile environment where members get angry, argue, and at times resort to physical violence. The families are beset with money problems, frequently missed meals or meals at strange times, important birthdays and holidays that are ruined by problems with the heavy drinker, and shame and embarrassment at their situation.

Family members often lie, deny, and make excuses so that strangers don't learn their secret of living with an alcoholic. The spouse and children may avoid making close friends and bringing people home, in order to keep the alcoholic and the problems caused by alcoholism from being exposed.

Children of alcoholics usually experience high levels of tension and stress. Many young children suffer the effects of intense anxiety and depression. Young children may show such symptoms as frequent crying, bedwetting, loneliness, fear of going to school, and nightmares.

Older COAs show other symptoms. Ninth-grader Peter avoids the other kids at school; at home he stays in his room watching television or sleeping. Nina, a high school senior, is a perfectionist who insists that everything she wears, eats, or does is ''exactly'' right; if not, she has a temper tantrum or grows sulky.

Many teenaged COAs cope by trying not to cause any upset in the family routine out of fear of setting off a drinking bout that might end with physical or sexual abuse. Because family life completely revolves around the alcoholic, children of alcoholics frequently grow up believing that nobody really loves them or cares what happens to them. Often they blame themselves or other members of their family for their parent's drinking behavior.

## WHY DO MANY COAS BECOME ALCOHOLICS?

For a combination of genetic and environmental reasons, COAs are at high risk of developing into alcoholics themselves. Studies show that sons of alcoholic fathers are four to five times more likely to become alcoholics than sons of nonalcoholic fathers, and daughters of alcoholic mothers are about three times more likely to turn to alcohol. Both boys and girls tend to become alcoholics themselves at a rate as much as five times higher than children of nonalcoholics.[4] However, even where other adults who are alcoholics care for the children—grandparents, aunts or uncles, or unrelated guardians—the children in these families are at risk of developing problems with alcohol.

Patterns of alcohol abuse and alcohol dependence vary among individuals in this group. Generally speaking, though, COAs who start drinking at a younger age pass more quickly through the stages of alcoholism than children who start later.

Some COAs become hooked on alcohol soon after taking their first drink. Right from the start they feel a powerful need to keep on drinking. Others either move gradually through the stages of increasing alcohol dependency or stop drinking altogether.

As yet, the process is not completely understood. But the effects of the early home environment, including family influences on drinking behavior, have been explored. Experts know that healthy development requires mastering emotional and social tasks at various ages throughout childhood. These tasks include learning how to share, to interact, to engage in problem-solving, and to separate from parents. These skills are accomplished through play and fun activities, exposure to recreational and cultural opportunities, and peer relationships. Because they may be deprived of many of these experiences, many children of alcoholics have difficulty growing in developmentally healthy ways.

### ? ? ?
## WHY DO SOME COAS NEVER BECOME ALCOHOLICS?

While many children develop serious problems due to parental alcoholism, some COAs function very well, despite family situations that put them at risk. Although about one-third of all alcoholics have one or more parents who are also alcoholic, less than half of children of alcoholics develop drinking problems, and only a portion of these develop alcohol dependency.[5]

A long-range study of COAs born on the island of Kauai found that 41 percent of the children had developed emotional problems by eighteen years of age, which is a high percentage. But, on the other hand, 59 percent did not develop problems.[6]

These "resilient" children, who survived growing up in an alcoholic home, shared several characteristics that contributed to their success. Among the most important of these traits are:

o the ability to obtain positive attention from other people
o the ability to communicate effectively with other people
o an average intelligence
o a caring attitude
o a desire to achieve
o a belief in self-help

Many children of alcoholics who never become alcoholics make positive adjustments to their families' alcoholism. Even COAs in high-risk environments with other sources of stress, including poverty, divorce, serious emotional problems, and histories of abuse and neglect, are able to overcome their painful beginnings and build healthy, fulfilling lives for themselves.

COAs who succeed are usually those who do not believe that they are the cause of the alcoholism in the alcoholic family member, or that they can cure or control it. They learn to cope with alcoholism at home by developing themselves, by getting involved in things that interest them, and by seeing life as really worth living despite the painful times and situations that they endure.

Therapists and others who work with COAs help them to see beyond their present circumstances. They try to instill a feeling of connectedness—to the community; to their ethnic, cultural, and religious heritages; and to nature, art, and history. Above all, they let them know that asking for help is a good thing to do, that it is a sign of strength not weakness.

### ? ? ?
## DO COAS DIFFER FROM CHILDREN OF NONALCOHOLICS?

Many school-aged COAs do poorly in school, even though they may be just as intelligent as children of nonalcoholics. Studies that compare the academic abilities and reasoning skills of COAs and children of nonalcoholics from middle-class backgrounds find no differences between the groups. Yet school records clearly show that COAs have many more academic difficulties, such as repeating a grade, failing to graduate from high school, and being referred to school psychologists.

Researchers suggest a probable cause. In general, alcoholic parents underestimate their own ability and their children's abilities to function well in the day-to-day world. This lack of confidence may have a negative impact on the children's self-esteem and their future well-being.

The stress of the home environment also may contribute to problems in school. Some children of alcoholics have difficulty relating to their teachers, other students, and the school community in general. Others become very tense and anxious due to a fear of failing.

Children from homes with alcoholic parents often demonstrate more behavior problems. These children exhibit such problems as lying, stealing, fighting, truancy, and school behavior problems, and they are often diagnosed as having conduct disorders. Often they cover up their real feelings by pretending they don't care. Teachers have rated COAs as significantly more overactive and impulsive than children of nonalcoholics.

Investigators have measured the emotional problems of children in different family situations: families of relapsed alcoholics, families with a recovering parent, and families with no alcohol problem. As expected, the children of relapsed alcoholics showed higher levels of anxiety and depression than children from the homes with no alcoholic. Emotional functioning, however, was much the same among the children of recovering and normal parents. The conclusion is that the emotional stress of parental drinking on children lessens when parents stop drinking.

A general characteristic of many COAs is poor verbal skills: they have trouble expressing themselves, both in speech and in writing. This difficulty in expression may account, in part, for their poor achievement in school. Problems with verbal skills not only lower their school performance, but also interfere with an ability to develop and sustain friendships.

The United States government survey report, ''Exposure to Alcoholism in the Family,'' supports the idea that exposure to alcoholism in the home affects educational success. Over 30 percent of young women who had not completed high school had grown up with an alcoholic, while only about 20 percent of young women who had attended college came from alcoholic homes. For young men, 23 percent who had not graduated from high school had been exposed to alcoholism, compared to 16 percent who had attended college.[7]

Research on children of alcoholics is still in its beginning stages. And many of the studies suggest that a variety of differences exist among COAs. Although few generalizations apply to all children who grow up with alcoholic parents, we now know that many children of alcoholics are at equal risk for alcoholism as youngsters growing up in troubled, but nonalcoholic, homes.

??? 

## WHAT ARE THE DIFFICULTIES OF LIVING WITH AN ALCOHOLIC PARENT?

Among the most commonly described difficulties of living with an alcoholic parent is inconsistency. When a parent drinks, his or her behavior and expectations may change from day to day, or even from hour to hour.

Most days when Judy, a ninth grader, comes home from school she finds her mother busy preparing dinner or perhaps doing the family ironing. But some days Judy discovers a completely different mother at home—someone dozing in front of the television, unable to stand up and slurring her words when she tries to speak. On the days following the drinking episodes, Judy's mom has difficulty remembering what happened.

Mitch has had similar experiences with his alcoholic father. Most of the time, Mitch's dad lets him practice his electric guitar in their basement. But every once in a while, usually on days when he has had a particularly large amount to drink, Mitch's dad storms down to the basement, shouts, and threatens to break the guitar if the playing doesn't stop.

Many COAs never know what to expect from one moment to the next. The alcoholic parent can suddenly change from being loving to angry—regardless of what the child is doing. This makes it very hard for COAs to trust their parents. Unable to guess what their parents' mood will be, they often do not know how they should behave. Repeated delays and disappointments, broken promises, and outright lies often lead to problems in trusting others or developing close relationships.

Inconsistent child-rearing practices can lead to confusion and immaturity. Children of alcoholics frequently have real problems distinguishing between sober parental concerns and expectations, and the extreme or unreasonable demands they make when drunk.

The disruptions caused by having an alcoholic in the family make it very difficult to keep to a regular daily schedule. Most young children find it very important to have a routine that stays the same from day to day. Constantly changing bedtimes and mealtimes, sudden mood swings, and unpredictable behavior can cause fear and uncertainty in children of all ages.

Teenagers may feel embarrassed for and about their alcoholic parent. Most adolescents want to have a "normal" family, a family like their friends' families. Living in a family where one of the parents has a drinking problem often means that the family is not like other families, that there is something "wrong" with them. " 'Nice' people from good neighborhoods aren't supposed to have drinking problems," says one adolescent. And so older children frequently resort to hiding their personal and family turmoil from the outside world.

At the same time, embarrassed parents may give

their child the message that there is a terrible secret at home. The ashamed child does not want to betray the family and hesitates to invite friends home. Also, the young person is afraid to ask anyone for help, realizing that confiding in an outsider would reveal the carefully hidden problem of alcoholism at home.

Many adolescents in alcoholic homes work very hard to avoid calling any attention at all to their families. Because of these feelings of shame and embarrassment, these young people are likely to stay isolated. They may even spend time away from home in order to avoid having to face the problems brought about by an alcoholic parent.

Adolescent children of alcoholics worry a lot—about themselves, their parents, and their family life. They worry that the nonalcoholic parent may get a divorce and leave the alcoholic parent, that the alcoholic parent's drinking may result in loss of a job, that this parent will be hurt in an accident or get sick because of the alcohol. To make it worse, the child often feels somewhat guilty because of the mistaken belief that he or she created the drinking problem, and also feels helpless to change the situation.

Out of these various concerns come strong feelings of anger and betrayal. "How can she do this to me?" "Why can't he stop drinking and be like everybody else?" The child feels angry at the alcoholic parent for drinking and angry at the nonalcoholic parent for not putting an end to the drinking. Sometimes, children of alcoholics turn this pent-up anger against others. They lose their tempers with teachers, friends, teammates, and others, simply because they are angry with their parents.

The children's anger often leaves the drinking and nondrinking parents confused and unhappy. Sometimes the nonalcoholic parent tries especially hard to win the child's favor by severely criticizing the alcoholic parent or by giving the child things to do, like taking care of the other children, something that is really the responsibility of the alcoholic.

Due to the social and psychological difficulties of living with an alcoholic, the COAs also tend to adopt a distinct role within the family. Dr. Claudia Black, herself the daughter of alcoholic parents and a leading therapist and national advocate of child rights, points to four common roles that children assume in alcoholic households:[8]

*The Responsible Child.* Some older children in alcoholic families take on the role of the parent, feeding and caring for younger brothers and sisters and acting like a responsible parent.

Tom, age thirteen, is an example of a "responsible child." His father had a bad drinking habit—and his mother often joined the father in his heavy drinking. Tom had three younger siblings—Patty, Mary, and Tim. Every morning, often while both parents were still asleep, Tom helped them get dressed, prepared their cereal for breakfast, and made sure they got to school on time.

*The Adjuster Child.* Some children simply accept the behavior of the drinking parent and respond to the situation by becoming quiet and withdrawn.

By the time she entered junior high school, Ellen realized that her father was different from most other fathers, that he had a serious drinking problem and was indeed an alcoholic. She pleaded with him and begged him to stop his drinking, to no avail.

At first Ellen made deals with her father. "Stop drinking and I'll do extra homework—I'll do the dishes every night, I'll wash the car." Eventually she gave up trying to break his habit. She withdrew into herself. She hardly spoke at all, gave up most of her friends, and spent most of her time alone. When asked what was wrong, she merely said, "You wouldn't understand."

*The Acting-Out Child.* Some children adopt a strategy of creating problems of their own at home and school. Unconsciously they hope to draw attention to themselves and away from the usual focus of the family's concerns by precipitating a crisis situation.

Jeff did not seem affected by his father's drinking problem until fifth grade. Then, gradually his grades went down and he had a number of run-ins with his teacher and fights with other children in his class. Within a year, the number—and seriousness—of the incidents picked up and Jeff was suspended from school for bad behavior. Eventually he stopped going to school altogether.

*The Placater Child.* Some children ignore their own sadness and pain and devote themselves to trying to comfort others.

Joey played this role in the home that he shared with his alcoholic father, mother, and three younger siblings. When his father started to pick on his mother, he became the peacemaker. When his sisters or brother got depressed he took them for a bike ride or tried to cheer them up any way he could. Over and over, he would try to help patch things up when it looked as though everything was coming apart.

According to Dr. Black, COAs become experts at playing the roles they take on. She suggests that they become so skillful in dealing with and handling alcoholics that it leads many to marry problem drinkers. As adults, these children of alcoholics continue to play the same part with their spouses as they played as children with their parents.

? ? ?

## CAN OTHERS HELP THE CHILDREN OF ALCOHOLICS?

Migs Woodside, of the Children of Alcoholics Foundation, has prepared a list of nine steps for friends or relatives to follow in trying to help the COAs cope with their situation.

**1.** Be a good listener. Let the child tell the story without comment or interruption. Accept what the young person says. Don't question any of the statements.

**2.** Encourage the child's friendship. Invite the child for an occasional meal or to go along on a short trip. This is especially valuable around holiday times when the stress in the alcoholic family is greatest.

**3.** Offer the child a haven, a quiet, safe place to come during family fights or whenever the child wants to spend some time away.

**4.** Give the child your phone number and offer to drive him or her when the parent has been drinking and cannot drive.

**5.** Suggest that the child find others who are sympathetic and understanding, such as neighbors, teachers, relatives, who could be there to help when there is a family crisis.

**6.** Explore pastimes and hobbies that will catch the interest and enthusiasm of the child.

**7.** Help the child to learn more about alcoholism and alcoholics by suggesting books and articles to read.

**8.** Guide the child to find professional help— through school, church, synagogue, or a community center—or to find a self-help group, such as Alateen or Al-Anon.

**9.** Do all that you can to lessen the child's feelings of guilt. Convince the child that the alcoholism is not his or her fault.

### ? ? ?
## WHAT CAN YOU DO IF YOU'RE A CHILD OF AN ALCOHOLIC?

The first thing that experts say to do is realize that thousands of others across the country have the same problem as you. You are not alone; many just like you wish that they had a family where drinking was not a problem.

The most difficult next step in doing something about the problem is to begin to communicate the sadness and anger that you feel. Find someone to talk to about it— an interested teacher, friend, or relative. Even though, out of love and fear, you may think it best to keep family problems to yourself, keeping everything secret and locked up inside yourself can hurt you in the long run.

If you believe that you are the child of an alcoholic remember that you are not to blame. Your parents have a problem and the best way you can help them is to help yourself.

A wide variety of warning signs may signal a drinking problem at home. These include: failure in school or truancy; withdrawal from classmates and former close friends; frequent physical complaints, such as headaches or stomachaches; overly aggressive play; and delinquent behavior, such as lying, shoplifting, and violence.

Healing can begin once you confront and express the guilt and fear you have worked so hard to cover up. Since learning about alcoholism is important to the process, you might want to participate in a group therapy or self-help program, such as Al-Anon or Children of Alcoholics. Other therapy programs include dietary changes (particularly low-fat, low-sugar diets) and stress-reduction techniques.

Basically, you must work to develop a healthy sense of self-esteem—free of guilt, fear, and blame—and begin to see yourself as okay even when those around you are not. Before you can trust others you must learn to trust yourself.

When President Bill Clinton was a teenager he had an encounter with his stepfather, Roger Clinton, that he said changed his life forever. Roger Clinton was an alcoholic who was gentle by day but violent and abusive after drinking bourbon at night. After one particularly violent incident of domestic conflict, Bill Clinton warned his stepfather that he had better not hit either his mother or brother again or he would do something to make him stop. Although his stepfather continued to drink bourbon, Roger Clinton never struck a family member again. By confronting the object of his pain, Bill Clinton had taken a big step toward healing himself.

# 6

# ADULT CHILDREN OF
# ALCOHOLICS

Did you know?

o Forty-three percent of the adult population in the United States has been exposed to alcoholism in the family.[1]

o A recent study found that 59 percent of female adult children of alcoholics reported an eating disorder, compared with 19 percent of the control group.[2]

o Fifty percent of adult children of alcoholics marry alcoholics.[3]

? ? ?

## WHO ARE THE ADULT
## CHILDREN OF ALCOHOLICS?

Today, when people speak of adult children of alcoholics (ACOAs), they refer to adults who were raised in alcohol-dependent homes. ACOAs are not spouses of alcoholics and they may or may not have drinking problems themselves. Adult children of alcoholics are simply individuals who may have adjustment problems due to their background and experience growing up in homes where alcohol was abused.

Most case histories of ACOAs describe childhoods full of neglect and mistreatment by the alcoholic parents. As children, they led unusually chaotic and very far from normal lives. The typical adult child of alcoholics was promised many things that he or she never received. Lying, in the form of denial, cover-ups, and inconsistencies were a basic part of family life. During childhood, these ACOAs were constantly criticized and reproached for not doing better. They lived with parents who varied from warm and loving to cold and distant when under the influence of alcohol.

Most experts believe that adult children of alcoholics have unique emotional patterns and problems that come from their childhood experiences. These include: feeling different from others, protecting themselves by lying and suppressing their feelings, being reluctant to stand up for themselves, and withdrawing from close relationships. Having learned these defensive behaviors as children, ACOAs tend to repeat them in adulthood, usually without realizing the connection. Sometimes these emotional problems surface only when they become adults.

According to these experts, growing up in a mixed-up, dysfunctional family makes many grown children of alcoholics unsure of what constitutes normal reactions and relationships. "After spending a whole lifetime covering up in order not to be found out," says one, "I'm suffering from a great deal of confusion. I just don't know what normal is."

An estimated 10 to 15 percent of all adult children of alcoholics seek help for their problems.[4] While accounts from both professional treatment and self-help programs make it appear that all ACOAs are affected by family alcoholism, the extent of the problem is far from certain.

### ? ? ?
## WHAT ARE THE SIMILARITIES AMONG ADULT CHILDREN OF ALCOHOLICS?

Accounts of ACOAs point out a number of very common problems, such as depression, aggression, impulsive behavior, and antisocial acts. Some other studies tell of an inability to avoid many kinds of substance abuse, great difficulty in establishing and maintaining good, healthy relationships with others, frequent failures as parents themselves, and a history of poor career choices. Of the many lists of characteristics, however, almost everyone names a particularly negative self-image as the key factor underlying many of the more troublesome behaviors of ACOAs.

People with a poor self-image have a tendency to internalize their childhood feelings of worthlessness, failure, and incompetence. Take Alan, for example, a thirty-year-old adult child of an alcoholic. Alan is the head of a small manufacturing company in New Haven, Connecticut. Despite his present success, however, Alan considers himself a disaster. When asked to explain, he says, "As a child, whatever I did was not quite good enough. No matter how hard I tried, I should have tried harder." He still feels this way today.

Like some other ACOAs, Alan was deeply troubled by his father's drinking problem. He tried to win his father's love and attention by becoming a super-student, a super-athlete, and a super-son. In truth, he did remarkably well. He attended honor classes in school, was quarterback on the football team, and won a scholarship to an outstanding college; in addition, he was a most helpful and considerate son. Yet nothing he did ever seemed to be enough.

More often than not, especially when he was on one of his drinking binges, Alan's dad was barely aware of Alan's existence and frequently got very angry with Alan for some imagined failing on his part. Now Alan plays that role with his own child.

Adult children of alcoholics also have problems with family responsibility, loyalty, and intimacy. Many grew up in homes with adults unable to be good parents and incapable of fulfilling their obligations to their children. Furthermore, their parents were often unwilling—or unable—to be frank and honest with each other and set poor adult role models for their children to follow.

Stanley is a typical adult child of alcoholics who still lacks maturity in forming and maintaining relationships. As a young man, Stanley dropped out of college. Throughout his work career, he rarely held a job for more than a year, always laying the blame on his bosses for some fault or another.

Stanley has few close friends because each time he meets someone new, he does something that breaks off the relationship. Stanley attributes each setback or failure to the people around him; it never occurs to him that he may be the one at fault. Without healthy relationships with other people to build on, adult children of alcoholics, like Stanley, frequently have difficulty interacting with others.

Doris's story is a little different. She grew up in a home where her father had a serious drinking problem and her mother suffered beatings and other domestic violence. After a very unhappy childhood, Doris became a teenaged bride right after graduation from high school.

Doris expected that her marriage would bring her some measure of security, but she soon found out otherwise. She discovered that she had married an alcoholic like her father. Not having had any idea of how to make her marriage work, Doris became unreasonably demanding and possessive of her husband, following him around, listening in on his phone calls, and questioning him about how he spent his time and money.

When Doris's husband reacted with anger and annoyance, Doris withdrew and started her own drinking habit. When intoxicated, she would not go to work, shop, or prepare meals. Her husband began drinking more heavily and spending more and more time away from home. When he came back, the couple argued and fought. After some time, Doris went into therapy. She is receiving treatment for alcoholism problems that relate back to her experiences growing up in an alcoholic household.

Joseph A. Califano, former United States Secretary of Health and Human Services, points out some other interesting facts about adult children of alcoholics. He states that adult sons of alcoholics see doctors more often than those raised in nonalcoholic homes. Further, they have higher rates of such psychological or mental disorders as anxiety, depression, and introversion.[5]

Adult daughters of alcoholics tend to have more reproductive problems and see their gynecologists and obstetricians more often. In addition, these women have a higher rate of bulimia, an eating disorder characterized by consuming huge amounts of food very quickly in a single binge—and then forcing themselves to throw up.

Despite many troublesome personality traits, some ACOAs also emerge from childhood with some important strengths. Chiefly, the more fortunate know how to function well in crisis situations, how to make sure that the necessary tasks get done, and how to cope with adversity.

Many ACOAs perform very well on the job. True, they often don't get along with the other employees, but they can be counted on to accomplish their jobs in spite of confusion and setbacks.

? ? ?

## WHAT ARE THE DIFFERENCES AMONG ACOAS?

Adult children of alcoholics are the product of vastly different genetic and environmental factors. Birth order, sex, family dynamics, and their individual rates of growth and development all play major roles in shaping their personal characteristics. New research is now trying to determine how varying life experiences add to the diversity found among ACOAs.

Dr. Claudia Black, a most important writer and therapist, recognizes alcoholism as the main problem for ACOAs. But in her book, *Double Duty*, she offers this list of additional factors that must be considered in trying to help or treat adult children of alcoholics:

*Only children.*

*Children with two chemically dependent parents.*

*Children who suffer from physical and sexual abuse.*

*People of color.*

*Gays and lesbians.*

*The physically disabled.*

*Those with food addictions.*

*Those with chemical addictions.*

??? 

## WHAT ARE THE SIMILARITIES BETWEEN ACOAS AND ADULT CHILDREN OF NONALCOHOLICS?

Researchers recognize many similarities between the "laundry list" of problems for ACOAs and those of adult children who grew up in other kinds of troubled families. Feelings of insecurity, difficulty in trusting others, and a lack of faith in other people's motives, do not belong *only* to ACOAs. These are problems also common to many people who come from nonalcoholic, but troubled, homes.

When adults who grew up in a home with an alcoholic parent are compared with adults who grew up in a home with a schizophrenic mother, both groups show a very negative self-image. Also, the adult children of schizophrenics show symptoms—such as a limited ability to concentrate on a single subject or topic, an impaired ability to solve problems, and an angry, hostile attitude in communicating with others—that are similar to symptoms found in adult children of alcoholics. Further, there is a tendency for children of schizophrenics to develop the disease later on, much as children of alcoholics tend to become alcoholics later in life.

Thus, growing up in a troubled home—whether with alcoholism, schizophrenia, or any other serious problem—produces a number of somewhat similar conditions. Most important, according to Dr. Black, is the common denominator the groups share—a sense of personal loss. This feeling of loss, Dr. Black writes, may stem from physical abandonment, emotional abandonment, or both.[6]

Dr. Kenneth Sher, a psychologist at the University of Missouri, conducted a recent study in which he listed the traits of children of alcoholics. Then he asked 112 children of alcoholics and 112 children of nonalcoholics whether the traits applied to them. The results were surprising. Two-thirds of each group said the descriptions fit them well![7]

Dr. Sher's conclusion is that the traits usually used to describe ACOAs are so universal and vague that they apply to everyone and are not very useful. But others commenting on Dr. Sher's study say that the children of nonalcoholics who believed the traits applied to them may simply come from other kinds of troubled families.

# 7

# THE DYSFUNCTIONAL FAMILY

Did you know?

○ The divorce rate in alcoholic families is four times the national average.[1]

○ Ninety percent of all reported child abuse cases were from substance-abusing families.[2]

○ Twenty percent of alcoholic families have both parents addicted to alcohol or other drugs.[3]

## ? ? ?
## WHAT IS A DYSFUNCTIONAL FAMILY?

A dysfunctional family is one that doesn't work well as a social unit. As a result of alcoholism or some other basic problem, the family encounters a variety of difficulties, from paying its bills to getting along with family members and people outside the home. Basically, a dysfunctional family does not fully provide for either the physical or the psychological needs of its members.

In a dysfunctional family, the home atmosphere is usually extremely tense. Family members often explode in anger or frustration; parents and children share few out-of-home experiences and those they do share are seldom joyous occasions. Compared with nonalcoholic families, dysfunctional families of alcoholics have much lower levels of family togetherness and much higher levels of conflict.

Jane knows too well the problems of growing up in a dysfunctional alcoholic family. Some of her most painful early memories have to do with swimming, which she started when she was ten years old. She was most eager to compete and showed great sports talent. At first, her parents paid for private lessons and came to all her meets.

But then suddenly, her alcoholic father objected to her swimming. He tore up her awards and broke her trophies. He accused Jane of "getting too big for her britches," and "driving him to drink." He also forced her mother to stop taking her to practice sessions and meets.

In dysfunctional families, a single individual often dominates the family unit and tries to impose his or her ideas and values on everyone else. Often this person uses physical or mental abuse to accuse, control, and punish his spouse and children.

In the face of this assault by the alcoholic parent, children like Jane may lose all respect for the nonalcoholic parent for not "doing something" about the problem. This makes the situation within the family even worse. The bruises and pain of domestic violence usually heal and fade, but the abuse frequently leaves emotional scars on family members that last far longer.

One result of an overbearing alcoholic is that the spouse and children start to believe his accusations. They hold themselves responsible and blame themselves for what the alcoholic is doing. These feelings of guilt, the refusal to admit that alcohol is the real problem, and the fear of criticizing the alcoholic are all typical of dysfunctional families with alcoholism.

In a dysfunctional family, the family members protect their inner feelings. They only express "certain" feelings that they consider acceptable; they deny or bury all others. A sense of shame and embarrassment surrounds many subjects having to do with the problems in the family. And they are burdened with a load of family secrets.

Family members—especially children—may withdraw from social contacts and keep friends out of the home. They may try to hide or deny family problems and be afraid to seek help or support.

Most adolescents growing up in a dysfunctional family with an alcoholic parent are confused, ashamed, hurt, angered, and embarrassed by the parent's behavior. They want to love and help the parent, but have no idea what they can or ought to do. Society tells them that parents are supposed to take care of and guide their children. But children of alcoholics often feel the very opposite is true. They must protect and take care of the parents—a role they are not experienced enough to handle, and a role that makes their parents resentful and angry.

?  ?  ?

## WHAT IS A HEALTHY FAMILY?

While there is no such thing as a perfect family, one without any problems, experts agree on a number of the most important qualities found in the majority of healthy families.

The following list, adapted from Dr. Black's book, *Double Duty*, points out some of these characteristics:

In a normal or healthy family people feel free to talk about their inner feelings. All feelings are okay, and it is more important to express these feelings than to deny that they exist or to hide them.

People in the family accept each member's individual differences and believe that the person is more important than what he or she does.

75

Family members accept responsibility for their own actions and accept the consequences of what they do. There are clear rules and standards of behavior and outcomes are fair and predictable.

Parents and children love, enjoy, respect one another, and have a strong sense of self-esteem. They celebrate birthdays, holidays, and other important family events and milestones together. Even children with alcoholic parents are less likely to become alcoholics as adults when their parents consistently set and follow through on plans and maintain such rituals as holidays and regular mealtimes.

A series of studies of families in which one or both parents were alcoholics offers the best proof of the emotional advantages of family rituals. In the families studied, some family members helped themselves to food in the kitchen and then went off on their own to eat, while others used dinners as a time to get together. Those children, especially sons, that came from homes where family dinners and other rituals continued despite a parent's heavy drinking were less likely to become alcoholics or to marry alcoholics. "It's unclear," said Dr. Steven Wolin, leader of the research on family rituals, "whether the advantage comes from the rituals themselves, or whether the rituals are a marker of some other healthy capacity in family life."[4]

Until recently, most of the attention given to alcoholism focused on the alcoholics themselves—how alcohol was damaging their lives in terms of problems with work or health, car accidents, loss of family and friends, and so on. Today, experts are studying the effect of alcoholism on the family and on family processes in the home.

Researchers have found that at least four other people are affected by the behavior of every problem drinker. That means that another 76 million people are affected by alcohol, even if they do not drink themselves. And, certainly a good percentage of this 76 million are members of the immediate families of the alcoholics.[5]

Of course 76 million people make up a rather diverse group. Yet despite their differences, the families of alcoholics do have some characteristics in common with other dysfunctional families.

### ? ? ?
## HOW DOES ALCOHOLISM AFFECT THE DYSFUNCTIONAL FAMILY?

All too often, children of alcoholics in dysfunctional families adopt the motto—"Don't talk, don't trust, and don't feel."[6] When this attitude is combined with the stigma of alcoholism, it virtually eliminates any willingness to speak to others about the problem or to get help from outside the family.

As the pattern of secrecy develops, the family becomes more and more isolated. The children in dysfunctional families find it increasingly difficult to become involved in relationships and activities outside the family. In addition to this social isolation, the children find there are fewer and fewer child-parent activities. Children's experiences with inconsistency, broken promises, unpredictable behavior, and embarrassing incidents result in disappointment and anger.

In the dysfunctional alcoholic family, the child's need for love, support, and encouragement is frequently ignored or forgotten in the endless tug-of-war between the family and alcoholism. With few good role models to demonstrate how to express emotions in a positive way, the children adapt as best they can to the chaos and turbulence in the home.

Children who feel trapped by the stress of being part of a dysfunctional family may react in a number of ways: do poorly in school, suffer depression, behave aggressively, or become alcoholics themselves. Many parents are often not aware that alcohol is the most abused drug among young people, nor do they realize that both overly-strict and overly permissive homes can lead to alcohol dependency in children.

Children raised in dysfunctional alcoholic families see themselves and their life experiences differently than children raised in healthy families. Take this experiment in which children of alcoholics were shown three drawings of families:

**1.** A family talking and sitting close together.
**2.** A family talking, but not sitting close together.
**3.** A family that is not talking and not sitting close together.

When asked to choose the drawing that best describes their families, most children of alcoholics chose the picture in the last category—not talking and not sitting close together.[7]

Excessive drinking may affect the spouse of the alcoholic most of all. He or she often develops many abnormal patterns of feeling and behavior, such as strong feelings of resentment against the mate, equally powerful feelings of self-pity for the misery caused by the alcoholic, a willingness to lie and make excuses for the partner's drinking, and a general avoidance of social contacts outside the marriage. In extreme cases, the nonalcoholic spouse may suffer complete exhaustion and become physically or mentally ill.

The spouse often has to assume the roles of both parents. When this happens, new and unhealthy family patterns develop as family responsibilities shift from two parents to one parent and the children.

According to some, the dysfunctional household is usually more disrupted if the mother is the alcoholic parent—assuming she is the children's primary caregiver. Whether the mother, the father, or both parents are alcoholic, the neglect and abuse of the children is staggering. Indeed, it has been said, "Outside of residence in a concentration camp, there are very few sustained human experiences that make one the recipient of as much sadism as does being a close family member of an alcoholic."[8]

### ? ? ?
## WHAT IS DENIAL?

Denial is central to alcoholism; it keeps alcoholics from admitting to themselves or others that it is alcohol that is at the core of their problem.

In the early stages of alcoholism, drinkers deny that they have a problem and usually become angry if others express concern over their drinking behavior. Even during the later phases of alcoholism, when the drinker clearly has lost control over his or her drinking, there is still likely to be denial that alcohol is a problem. In part this is because physical or psychological dependence on a drug makes it almost impossible to be honest.

But alcoholics are not the only ones who deny a drinking problem. Members of dysfunctional families use denial to let them look for some other reason, often something they have done, to explain the drinker's alcohol dependency.

Diane says, "After my two older sisters were born, my father really wanted a boy. Then I was born—and he still didn't have a son. I think that's one of the reasons he drinks so much."

Arthur says, "I know Dad was always a heavy drinker. But if Mom hadn't left him and gotten the divorce, I'm sure he would have straightened out and gotten sober."

Grace says, "In one year they built a new highway, my father's motel on the old road went bust, and I was hit by a car that put me in the hospital for seven months. That's why Mom started drinking. And she has never stopped!''

At first, denial is understandable because every family loves and wants to protect its members. But as the disease progresses, there comes a time when the family becomes very negatively affected. As family members deny the obvious and struggle to look good for outsiders, their behavior can trigger a number of emotional problems in the children of the family.

Treating children of alcoholics is often difficult because they deny that there are troubles at home. The drinking parent insists that he or she does not have a problem. And the children learn early that the one thing most likely to cause distress and upset in the home is to discuss the problem with outsiders. This makes it all the harder for therapists to help the children recognize the true nature of the problem and to take steps to improve the situation.

Denial sometimes makes it possible for a dysfunctional family to hide their drinking problems for a long time and to delay treatment. Using denial, dysfunctional families can remain in the same unhappy situation for years.

??? 

## WHAT IS CODEPENDENCY?

Codependency is a term used to describe the unhealthy reactions of the spouse, children, other relatives, employers, and friends to the alcoholic. Codependents let the alcoholic shape their behavior and destroy their self-esteem so that they end up contributing to the alcoholic's alcohol habit. They also often become so involved with the drinker that they ignore their own needs and desires.

Take the example of Marty, the drinking member of

a dysfunctional family. His wife and children, as seems quite natural, wanted to protect him. But in the process, they became codependents. By taking over his responsibilities and covering up for him, they stopped caring for themselves, and made it easier for him to continue drinking.

Marty was a self-employed accountant. When his income started to drop due to heavy drinking, Carol, his wife, went to work full-time. The two teenaged children also worked after school and on weekends. Whenever Marty was too drunk or too hung over to keep business appointments, Carol lied and said that he was sick. The children met their dates outside the home and always made excuses when their dad did not show up at school affairs. Carol punished, bribed, and threatened Marty. She hid or dumped out the contents of bottles. She even started to drink along with him.

This pattern of codependent behavior became very hard on Carol and the kids. In addition to feeling depressed and withdrawing from social contacts, they started complaining of physical ailments, ranging from headaches and back pains to sleeplessness and frequent stomachaches.

Shielding Marty from the difficulties caused by drinking weakened his desire to do something about his problem. The scoldings only increased his guilt and made him rely on alcohol even more. And drinking with him threatened to give Carol a drinking problem herself.

In a recent study, Dr. Jeff Greenberg, a psychologist at the University of Arizona, attempted to find out if adult children of alcoholics prefer mates who share the destructive traits of their parents. His results showed that at least some adult children of alcoholics tend to marry partners who are as demanding and self-centered as their drinking parent. Having learned to get love by meeting the demands of a self-centered parent as children, Dr. Greenberg said, "they get the same warm feelings when they meet the demands of a manipulative partner."[9]

Codependents need experts to help them cope with alcoholism. They need to learn that they are not responsible for the alcoholic and that they are not able to stop the alcoholic from drinking. Forcing the alcoholic to make promises that can't be kept only leads to failure, lies, and distrust. Breaking codependency by making basic changes in the way they treat the alcoholic is often the family's best first step in turning things around.

# **PREVENTION**

Did you know?

○ Illnesses, lost production, and property damage caused by alcoholism cost $42 billion a year.[1]

○ Drunk-driving accidents result in the deaths of 25,000 men, women, and children every year.[2]

○ One out of every two murders, rapes, robberies, and assaults takes place soon after drinking.[3]

? ? ?

## CAN ALCOHOLISM BE PREVENTED?

The goal of prevention is to avoid any drinking that may produce a problem—social or medical, mild or severe. Prevention also aims to reduce all the harmful effects of alcohol. This includes everything from stopping children from taking their first drink to handling the serious problems of alcohol abusers and alcohol-dependent persons. Legislators, law enforcement officials, health professionals, educators, business leaders, and concerned citizens play a part in this aspect of alcohol prevention.

Just as alcoholism has many causes, experts now know that prevention has many approaches. These different ways involve everything from providing public information and education, to limiting the availability of alcoholic beverages, to working for basic social changes.

Researchers try to identify children at the greatest risk

for alcoholism. They consider the most important factor, which is genetic. As we said, children of alcoholics seem more likely to develop a drinking habit than others.

Certain psychological and/or social factors also signal children at high risk. The main ones are stress, depression, low self-esteem, antisocial behavior, difficulty in school, and social isolation. People with one or more of these symptoms are in some danger of abusing alcohol or becoming alcohol-dependent.

Experts consider abstinence, or not drinking at all, to be the best way to avoid alcoholism and the damaging effects it may have on the brain, liver, and rest of the body—especially for children at high risk. Abstinence avoids any and all potential damage to personal, familial, and interpersonal relationships associated with serious drinking problems.

Over the years experts have proposed many prevention measures—from encouraging abstinence to passing laws controlling the manufacture and sale of alcoholic beverages. Some such laws in the United States date back to the mid-nineteenth century when thirteen states enacted legislation prohibiting people from making or selling liquor in those states. Eventually, these laws were repealed, leaving no legal restrictions on drinking, except for those communities that voted to become ''dry,'' that is, to prohibit any liquor in their localities.

In the early years of the twentieth century, a fresh outcry against the evils of alcohol resulted in the passage of the Eighteenth Amendment to the Constitution in 1917. This so-called Prohibition Amendment made it illegal to make, sell, or transport alcoholic beverages anywhere in the United States.

The Eighteenth Amendment cut down the amount of drinking in the country, but it also created many problems. Because Prohibition had never won widespread popular support, people did not obey the law and it became almost impossible to enforce. "Moonshiners" began making their own liquor; gangs of "bootleggers" smuggled in liquor from other countries and distributed the illegal liquor made here; and places to buy and drink liquor, called "speakeasies," sprang up everywhere. After fourteen years, the American public was fed up with Prohibition, and in 1933 Congress passed the Twenty-First Amendment, which repealed the Eighteenth Amendment and put an end to Prohibition.

Today prevention workers approach the problem in different ways, and the exact mix of methods is determined by the professionals running the various programs, the group with whom they are concerned, and the community in which they are working.

### ？ ？ ？
## WHAT ARE NEW WAYS OF PREVENTING ALCOHOLISM?

Four approaches prevail in most programs today. The major components are:[4]

**1.** Information and education
**2.** Skill building
**3.** Social support
**4.** Psychological assistance

Since most young people know very little—and sometimes have wildly mistaken ideas—about alcohol and alcoholism, many programs start with information and education. Counselors establish the vocabulary for discussion and explain the concept of alcoholism as a disease. By learning about the substance and its effects on mind and body, the young person is better able to understand the risk factors, and thereby avoid or resist the temptation or pressure of peers to drink.

The second aspect of prevention helps young people

to develop the skills they need to handle situations that might lead to drinking activity:

*"What do you say when your father, who is drunk, wants to drive you home?"*

*"How do you say 'No' without looking like a nerd when a friend offers you a drink?*

*"What do you do if you are invited to a party where everyone is drinking either wine or beer?"*

Through role-playing, decision-making, and problem-solving situations, experts give youths practice in handling peers as well as other influences that may lead to a drinking habit. Such skill building is particularly important to children of alcoholics, but is helpful to everyone growing up in a society where alcoholism is so widespread.

Social support is especially important to children in dysfunctional families who feel isolated because of alcoholism or some other problem in their families. Meeting people with similar problems removes much of the children's guilt and self-blame and helps them to cope better with their own difficulties.

Psychological assistance helps those beset by emotional and behavioral problems to improve the quality of their lives. The assistance deals with confronting confused feelings of love, hate, anger, guilt, pity, and embarrassment about personal problems and problems within the family.

??? 

## WHAT IS BASIC PREVENTION RESEARCH?

Basic prevention research explores the factors that put people at risk of developing problems with alcohol use.

These factors include such individual characteristics as age, gender, and family history; factors within the environment, such as family interaction and the workplace situation; where and when the drinking is usually done; and the price of alcohol. Basic prevention research provides facts and figures that researchers can then use to devise the most effective prevention strategies.

For example, fetal alcohol syndrome (FAS) is an extremely important topic today. Before taking steps to decide on the best approach to preventing or controlling this problem, the workers in the field need up-to-date answers to such questions as:

*At what age are women most likely to give birth to infants with FAS?*

*Did the mothers grow up in, or are they now members of, alcoholic families?*

*Is alcoholism a widespread problem among the mother's friends, fellow workers, or neighbors?*

*What are the specific drinking patterns of women at risk for having babies with FAS?*

*Which is the best way to reach the women at risk—TV, radio, magazine, or newspaper ads? Family doctors? Health center counselors or social workers? Schools or community centers? Or some other way?*

? ? ?

## WHAT IS APPLIED PREVENTION RESEARCH?

Applied prevention research measures the effectiveness of the various actions that are taken to avoid problems related to alcohol use. For example:

87

*The government passes a law raising the minimum drinking age. Does that cut alcohol abuse?*

*The police crack down on drunk drivers. How much effect does that have on alcoholics?*

*The school offers information and education programs. Do the students drink less as a result?*

One example of applied prevention research grew out of the finding that work environments can play a major role in promoting heavy alcohol consumption. Based on this research, some manufacturing plants began providing free hot lunches inside the plant to stop lunch hour and parking-lot drinking. Now applied prevention research workers are trying to determine how well this approach works in cutting alcohol consumption.

??? 

## DO LEARNING PROGRAMS
## PREVENT ALCOHOL ABUSE?

Education and early intervention help to avoid or lessen the impact of alcholism on the individual and on the family. Therefore, most prevention programs for young children take place in schools, as well as in YMCAs and YWCAs, recreational centers, and public housing developments. The programs strive to avoid or at least delay the onset of alcohol use by giving the young people information on alcohol-related topics. Young people learn positive alternatives to drinking, and strengthen skills that will help prevent alcohol abuse or dependence.

Prevention programs for young children based on social learning theory, sometimes labeled ''social influence'' programs, seem to show promising results. Such programs stress ways to refuse alcohol, correct unrealistic expectations about alcohol, alert young people to inaccurate messages about drinking from advertisements, movies, and television, and provide information about parental and other adult influences.

The programs try to improve general coping skills and thereby reduce factors like low self-esteem and lack of self-confidence, which may lead to alcohol use. The approach focuses on managing stress, clarifying values, making decisions, and setting healthy, reachable goals.

Professionals organize the main approaches to prevention around specific targets:

*The individual—increasing the individual's knowledge about alcohol, helping the individual resist peer pressure, explaining acceptable norms of behavior.*

*The family—improving the functioning of the family, developing parenting skills.*

*The peer group—altering antisocial peer behavior, building up resistance against peer pressure.*

*School—alcoholism education and enforcement of school policies against alcohol.*

*Community—combining the first three approaches into a community-wide approach.*

*National—a campaign launched against alcoholism at the highest levels of the federal government.*

One noteworthy example of successful prevention is the "Life Skills Training" program[5] developed for children in grades seven through twelve. The aim is to improve skills in making decisions, teach the effects of drug and alcohol abuse, and develop ways of coping with anxiety, communicating with peers and adults, enhancing one's self-image, and resisting peer pressure to use drugs or drink.

Another well-accepted program is family based, and combines social learning with helping to improve the way families manage their affairs. The program involves home visits by school personnel to bring parents and teachers closer together, parent training classes to develop parenting skills, and services to resolve conflicts over the child's school or home behavior.

? ? ?

## CAN PRICE INCREASES PREVENT ALCOHOL CONSUMPTION?

A promising line of prevention research studies the link between the price of alcoholic beverages and alcohol use. For example, how does the price of alcohol affect the number of car crashes? The results suggest that a higher price, such as one brought about by an increase in federal taxes, may lead to a drop in heavy drinking and in fatal crashes among youths. One study estimated that even a 10 cents per package increase in the price of six twelve-ounce cans of beer would reduce

> ○ the number of sixteen to twenty-one year olds who drink by about 11 percent
> ○ the number who drink two or three times a week by 8 percent
> ○ the number who consume three to five cans of beer on a typical drinking day by 15 percent[6]

As for fatal automobile crashes, the same study estimates that a doubling of the beer tax would reduce highway deaths among fifteen-to seventeen-year-old drivers by as much as 18 percent.

Higher prices for alcohol were also found to be linked to lower rates of heavy drinking in another way. Death from cirrhosis of the liver, an indicator of ten to twenty years of heavy drinking, was lower in states that raised taxes on alcohol compared to states that did not raise taxes.

## DO THE MEDIA
## AFFECT ALCOHOL USE?

No one has yet found a strong connection between alcohol advertising and alcohol consumption. In part, this may be because it is very difficult to study the effects of advertisements on alcohol-related problems under laboratory conditions. Researchers, however, now believe that advertising bans seem to have little impact on alcohol sales or use. And most experts agree that the impact of day-to-day exposure to advertising on young people seems small compared to the impact of other factors, such as peer pressure.

Cutting the use and glamorization of alcohol on television, however, and portraying realistically the negative outcomes of drinking may be useful prevention measures. Frequent drinking scenes in television dramas may promote the idea that drinking is the expected and appropriate thing to do in many situations. One laboratory study, for example, showed some children aged eight to eleven a popular television show with drinking scenes, and showed other children the same show with the drinking scenes cut out. Afterwards, all the children were asked to describe the best beverage to serve adults. More of the children who saw the drinking scenes named alcohol than did the children who viewed the same show without the drinking scenes.[7]

## WHAT PART DO MINIMUM DRINKING
## LAWS PLAY IN PREVENTION?

In the early 1970s, many states in the United States reduced the legal minimum drinking age from twenty-one to eighteen. The drop in age was followed by an increase in alcohol consumption and alcohol-related accidents among drivers in this age group. This result led the federal government to attempt to raise the legal drinking age to twenty-one as a way of cutting deaths due to alcohol consumption by those aged eighteen to twenty-one. To help persuade the states to set twenty-one as the minimum age, the federal government cut off national highway funds to states that did not comply. By 1988 all fifty states had set the legal minimum drinking age at twenty-one.

Recent evidence shows that changes in the legal drinking age have reduced auto deaths due to drinking and driving. Eighteen-and nineteen-year-old drivers in states that raised the minimum drinking age to twenty-one had an immediate 13 percent decrease in fatalities, which was maintained long after drinking-age changes went into effect.[8]

The legislation, however, does not seem to prevent drinking in youths below the minimum drinking age. Teenagers still manage to gain access to alcohol from bars and liquor stores that don't check the customer's age and from home liquor cabinets. While the laws may have affected the auto death rates due to alcohol consumption, they do not seem to have stopped many adolescents from drinking.

### ? ? ?
## DO DRINKING-AND-DRIVING LAWS PREVENT ALCOHOLISM?

Drinking-and-driving laws are based on the assumption that the threat of fines, imprisonment, or loss of license will prevent individuals from drinking and driving. Thus far, researchers conclude, these so-called deterrent strategies may be effective in the short-term but they do not seem to have lasting benefits. The problem seems to lie mostly in the difficulty of enforcing these laws.

Thirty-five states now have "dram shop" laws. These laws allow individuals injured by drivers who were served alcohol to the point of intoxication to sue the server of the alcohol for damages. A prevention program called server training tries to control drinking by teaching servers to detect potential intoxication based on the amount of alcohol consumed, the rate of consumption, and the sex and weight of the customer. Training the server may be a very effective prevention measure because servers often deal with drinkers immediately before they start driving.

In most states, drivers found guilty of driving while intoxicated (DWI) can choose to take part in alcohol education or rehabilitation programs as an alternative to fines, jail sentences, or the loss of drivers' licenses. The purpose is twofold: to give drunk drivers the knowledge they lack about the effect of alcohol on driving and about their own drinking habits; and to change and improve attitudes about drinking so as to decrease accidents caused by DWI.

When researchers compared drunk drivers referred to rehabilitation programs with those who were punished with a fine or jail term, they found that the latter group had fewer crashes. But neither policy had much effect on later arrests for DWI. Some experts now feel that the best approach would be to supplement legal penalties with education programs. For example, increased penalties for DWI have shown much less effect on nineteen- and twenty-year-old drivers than on those who are fifteen through eighteen years of age.[9] Further prevention research is needed on the various effects on driving and drinking due to differences in age, gender, and socioeconomic status.

? ? ?
## HOW CAN YOU PREVENT
## ALCOHOLISM?

All prevention methods come down to one person—the individual drinker. What can you do to prevent yourself from developing a problem with alcohol?

The first step in personal prevention of alcoholism is recognizing that alcohol is a drug and that its use includes certain potential risks. Avoiding drinking as well as knowing your family's history with alcohol and understanding the disease and its early symptoms can lessen the chances that you will suffer because of alcohol-related problems.

Someone asked eleven-year-old Brian why he started drinking alcohol. He said, "I just tried it because others were trying it. My friends all wanted me to drink. And I wanted to be part of the group."[11]

Studies find that by sixth grade, about one child in twenty is already experimenting with alcohol and other drugs.[10] Most young users say that they were first turned on to drugs by friends. Almost everyone who starts to drink does it with other people. Many children say "Yes" to alcohol so that they will be accepted by the people they know. Their friends are drinking and they don't want to feel left out.

In many cases drinking also begins at home. Often it is with permission from the adults who live there or visit. A young child is given a sip from someone's glass or decides to drink the leftovers of what was prepared for grown-ups. Children who come from homes where alcohol is used freely sometimes have a ready excuse for drinking. They point to their parents and say, "If they can do it, so can I." This also helps them feel less guilty about drinking.

Growing up means making your own choices. It means deciding when you want to go along with friends and parents and when you want to think for yourself. It means choosing what you believe is right for you, even if it's different from what others have chosen.

Here's a list of suggested ways that you can withstand the influence of friends and others who drink:

*Believe in yourself. If you feel good about yourself, you won't risk ruining your life.*

*Talk your way out of drinking situations. Saying no to alcohol in a firm and definite way usually does the trick.*

*Take yourself out of drinking situations. If you're in a group that's not right for you, decide where you would rather be and go there.*

*Avoid friends who drink. Experts find that children who break the rules look for others like themselves.*

*Talk to someone you trust. It usually helps to open up, especially if you feel unsure about drinking. Sharing your feelings with someone you know and trust restores your faith in others. It also helps to listen to others who have been in similar situations. Learn how they worked things out, what they know about alcohol, how they avoided peer pressure.*

*Keep in mind that most people know that drinking can be dangerous, especially when it starts at an early age. They may not approve of drinking, but they respect people who are honest and open about drinking problems.*

# 9
# TREATMENT AND RECOVERY

Did you know?

○ Between 50 and 75 percent of all alcoholics are able to recover from their addiction.[1]

○ That the cost of treating alcohol problems is one-tenth the current cost of alcoholism to society.[2]

○ Nearly 1.5 million clients were treated in 5,586 alcoholism treatment centers in a recent twelve-month period.[3]

? ? ?

## CAN ALCOHOLISM BE TREATED?

Treatment often includes two kinds of related help—help for the alcoholic and help for the family. The alcoholic needs to be able to gain control over his or her alcohol dependency while the spouse and children need to solve the personal, psychological, medical, and financial problems that frequently develop within the alcoholic family.

Sometimes, the first expert that the alcoholic and the family turn to for help is the family doctor, who can treat the physical problems related to alcoholism. Often, too, a member of the clergy spots the problem and attempts to deal with the alcohol-related difficulties. Both can counsel the alcoholic and family and refer the patient to others as needed.

Most often, though, the dependent drinker goes to

specialists who treat alcoholics. These specialists vary considerably in training and background. Generally called therapists or counselors, they include alcohol counselors, psychiatric social workers, psychologists, and psychiatrists.

Marriage and family counselors can help families cope with the tensions created in an alcoholic-centered home. School counselors can often provide information and support to adolescents who have family problems stemming from alcoholism. And therapists at hospitals, mental health centers, and state-run alcohol programs provide information and services for alcohol-related problems.

Some therapists will see the alcoholic once or twice a week while the alcoholic lives at home and continues his or her regular daily routine. Others work in institutions, such as hospitals or alcoholic treatment centers, where the alcoholic may spend a period of time while being helped to break the drinking habit.

Alcohol withdrawal is the first step in recovery for the alcoholic. Withdrawal varies from person to person and patients may experience none, some, or all of three major symptoms. First, there are signs and symptoms of restlessness, sweating, rapid heartbeat, raised blood pressure, tremors, and other related symptoms. Second, there may be seizures. And third, distorted perceptions and sensations may produce hallucinations, delirium, and disturbed sleep.

Opinions vary on which medications should be used to treat alcohol withdrawal and whether the alcoholic should go through withdrawal in a medical or a social setting. Some patients may need to be alcohol-free for at least four to six weeks after alcohol withdrawal to get the best results from therapy programs.

Recovery from alcoholism can last for the rest of

the alcoholic's life. Even after years without a drop of liquor, the alcoholic will refer to himself or herself as a "nondrinking" or "recovering" alcoholic. This is because alcoholism cannot be "cured" in the way some other illnesses are cured. In the opinion of most experts, alcoholics are alcoholic for life. Once an alcoholic has stopped drinking he can never have another drink without the symptoms of alcoholism recurring.

### ? ? ?
## WHAT IS FAMILY INTERVENTION?

Intervention is a family's way of helping heavy drinkers or individuals at high risk for alcoholism get into treatment. It is a process by which family members force alcoholics to face them and to hear how their drinking patterns, behaviors, and attitudes have affected each and every member of the family.

Someone in the family, usually the spouse, becomes the organizer or facilitator and arranges the gathering without the alcoholic really knowing its purpose. Then, after lunch or dinner (without alcohol), family members bring up specific drinking behaviors of the alcoholic that have caused embarrassment, danger, disappointment, or other trouble over the years. In addition to confronting the alcoholic and insisting on the truth about the drinking problem, the spouse, relatives, and friends, as a family group, set up the details for getting help.

Intervention works best if it coincides with a period of recuperation from a hangover, the period when most alcoholics feel remorseful and have a temporary lowering of the guard. Everyone tries to balance their harsh words with sincere words of love, affection, and hope.

Family intervention is based on a procedure that has been used in industry. In so-called constructive confrontation, supervisors use employers and others to face workers who are not performing well on the job and make them realize the specific work-related problems they have caused.

Specialists say that it is necessary to break down denials before treatment can be successful. Few heavy drinkers volunteer for alcohol intervention even though they may be having problems showing up for school or work, handling arrests for alcohol-related offenses, coping with abandonment by family members, and dealing with alcohol-caused physical complaints or accidents. When asked to volunteer for treatment, most alcoholics will insist that there is nothing really wrong or they will lie and try to keep up an illusion of normalcy. Family intervention, it is said, presents the alcoholic with a united front that weakens the denial and dishonesty that allow the habit to continue.

### ? ? ?
## CAN TALKING "CURE" ALCOHOLISM?

"Talking" therapy is sometimes used alone with alcoholic patients, but is more often part of group therapy or some other method. Therapists try to help clients to understand why they started drinking, what keeps them addicted to alcohol, and how they can find the means, within themselves, to break the dependency.

The therapist talks with the patient, and listens to what the patient has to say. Through talk, the therapist discovers more about the drinker and his or her problem. Was drinking a way to handle fear, or guilt, or anger? Did drinking start because of peer or family pressure? Was alcohol used to relax, cheer up, forget worries, and gain courage? Did drinking occur most when lonely, angry, or nervous? Was drinking the result of a poor self-image and a way of feeling better about oneself?

Most important, therapists work to make alcoholics confront their dependency and put an end to the denial, to themselves or others, that they have a drinking problem. Most professionals believe that alcoholics must face the reality of their problem before any behavioral changes can take place.

Talking cannot "cure" alcoholism, but it can lead to recovery from its harmful effects.

### ? ? ?
## WHAT IS BEHAVIOR THERAPY?

Therapists use behavior therapy, or behavior modification, in treating alcoholism. Here the therapist does not focus only on the root causes of alcoholism. Rather, the main aim is to get the clients to change their behavior—to stop abusing alcohol and to replace the old, unwanted behavior (heavy drinking) with a new, much more desirable behavior (sobriety).

Basically, behavior therapy rewards desired behavior and punishes undesirable behavior. The rewards and punishments vary with the individual and with the setting. A reward might be money or special privileges for each alcohol-free day. The punishment might be the loss of money or withdrawal of privileges whenever the person takes a drink.

Aversion therapy is somewhat related to behavior therapy. This treatment gets the alcoholic to associate imagined drinking with unpleasant experiences such as nausea. One study used three groups of patients with a history of alcohol dependence. Group 1 saw scenes of nausea and vomiting caused by drinking; Group 2 saw the same scenes accompanied by horrible odors; and Group 3 saw other disturbing outcomes of drinking. Eighteen months later, all three groups showed considerable improvement compared to groups without aversion therapy.[4]

## ARE THERE DRUGS
## TO TREAT ALCOHOLISM?

For the last twenty years doctors have used drugs such as Librium and Valium among others as medications for alcohol withdrawal. These drugs help manage the symptoms of withdrawal and prevent the life-threatening delirium tremens (DTs).

Some treatment methods use prescribed drugs to foster sobriety. These drugs produce an unpleasant reaction when combined with alcohol. The most popular of these substances is probably Antabuse, the trade name for disulfiram, which has been used since the 1950s. If alcohol abusers drink alcohol within five days after taking Antabuse, they experience headaches, difficulty in breathing, vomiting, heart palpitations, dizziness, and double vision. Antabuse therapy is rarely used alone; it is almost always combined with one of the talking therapies.

Scientists have long believed that some people become alcoholics because of an imbalance in certain chemicals in the brain. These individuals are generally very anxious and worried or extremely restless and nervous. Liquor eases their anxiety and calms their restlessness. This sets up a tremendous desire, or even need, for more alcohol to relieve their discomfort.

In the 1990s, researchers began to follow a new and exciting direction in the use of drugs to help such problem drinkers. Take a case reported by Dr. Howard Moss, a psychiatrist at the University of Pittsburgh.[5] The patient was extremely high-strung from the time he was a young boy. His anxiety grew more severe when he entered junior high, and it became even worse whenever he was around girls.

By high school, the young man had learned that a few drinks of alcohol relaxed him, and let him be charming and funny with members of the opposite sex. Since his father was an alcoholic, he had no trouble getting all the alcohol he wanted at home.

In college he was drinking almost daily, before any social encounter as well as before classes. By the time he got a job as an accountant, he was drinking all day long. Discovered with alcohol on his breath, he was fired and came to Dr. Moss for treatment.

Dr. Moss found that the patient had a low level of the brain chemical gamma-aminobutyric acid (GABA). Research had previously shown that GABA is involved in feelings of anxiety; the less GABA activity in the brain, the greater the anxiety. In addition, Dr. Moss had made two findings about GABA and alcohol. First, alcohol makes the brain cells that take in GABA less able to receive the chemical. This makes the GABA become more active in the brain, which relieves the anxiety and tension. When the GABA level rises, the anxiety level drops. Further evidence supports the finding of a link between GABA deficiency and alcoholism. The sons of alcoholic fathers were shown to have less GABA than sons of fathers who did not have drinking problems. When the sons of alcoholics had a drink of alcohol, though, their GABA levels rose to normal levels.

Another case of Dr. Moss's shows the connection between restlessness and a chemical imbalance. This patient was hyperactive from the time he was in grade school. He seldom paid attention in class, was the school bully, cursed his teachers, and was finally suspended for smoking in sixth grade. He ran away from home for a week when he was twelve; at fifteen he dropped out of school to join a gang and spent his time fighting and in petty crime, along with drinking and drug use. Jailed at age seventeen, he took a series of menial jobs on his release, while continuing his habit of drinking two six-packs of beer every evening.

103

When he was twenty-four his girlfriend, who could no longer put up with his drinking and his wild, violent behavior, threw him out. That's when he entered treatment with Dr. Moss. Dr. Moss found two irregularities in his brain chemicals. He had low levels of both serotonin and monoamine oxidase. Studies have shown that a deficiency of serotonin leads to hyperactivity, aggressive behavior, and violence. Other studies have shown a connection between lower monoamine oxidase and people who like taking risks and looking for thrills and excitement. In this patient's case, the only way he knew to control himself and curb his violent and thrill-seeking desires was with alcohol.

Dr. Moss's conclusion? "They [alcoholics] drink to calm themselves."

As a result of such findings, the search is now on for drugs that will adjust the levels of certain brain chemicals. Researchers also want to discover when and how to use these drugs to prevent the development of an addiction to alcohol.

? ? ?

## WHAT IS FAMILY AND GROUP THERAPY?

Family therapy is a type of treatment that involves the alcohol abuser and the members of his or her family. Since individual drinking problems affect the whole family, and the behavior of the family contributes to the alcoholic's continuing dependency, treating alcoholism is truly a family matter.

Family therapists treat the whole family together—in the same room and at the same time. Everyone works together to resolve conflicts and misunderstandings. Skilled therapists can help each family member to know the others better, to better understand their needs, fears, hopes, and methods of coping with problems. By clarifying issues, by interpreting patterns of behavior, and by offering suggestions, the therapist can resolve many of the factors that have been tearing the family apart and help the family work together to make life better for everyone.

The majority of alcoholics—after individual therapy or right from the start—enter group therapy. The goal is to help people with alcohol dependencies achieve sobriety and improve their life-styles. Alcoholics join a number of other recovering alcoholics in sessions with a group leader. Being with other people in a similar situation, hearing their stories, learning about their successes and failures, and getting their reactions to personal stories can be very helpful in gaining control over a drinking problem.

Many therapists, early in the treatment, try to establish a few basic ideas in the family members:

**1.** You are not the cause of the alcoholism. Alcoholics drink because of themselves, not because of anyone else.

**2.** You can't control the person's drinking. The desire to stop drinking has to come from within the drinker. It cannot be forced on the drinker by someone else—no matter how much the drinker cares for that person and wants to please him or her.

**3.** You can't cure the drinking problem. Only the alcoholic who is motivated to come to treatment and stay with it once there can recover from alcoholism.

Although exact figures are hard to come by, experts estimate that over 50 percent of alcoholics recover after treatment. Patients in recovery have broken the pattern of alcohol dependency, reestablished themselves as family members, and become able to be productive in work or at school. Temporary relapses and setbacks may occur, but the person is able to return to sobriety.

? ? ?

## WHICH ORGANIZATIONS GIVE FREE HELP?

The oldest, best-known, and most successful nationwide self-help organization of recovering alcoholics is Alcoholics Anonymous (AA). AA holds that alcoholism is a chronic disease, from which the alcoholic never fully recovers, but that the members of AA have the power to control their drinking. The group holds regular meetings, and uses volunteers to help the alcoholic recover. In addition to being the preferred way of combatting alcoholism for many, AA is very often an important part of the other therapies.

Al-Anon is another organization closely tied to AA. It offers fellowship and help for families and friends of alcoholics.

Alateen is also associated with AA and Al-Anon. It is a voluntary program for young men and women, ages twelve to twenty, with an alcoholic family member, relative, or friend. It offers friendship, information, and help with alcohol-related problems.

Al-Anon and Alateen usually meet at the same place—such as a church hall or schoolroom—and at the same time. But their meetings are separate—adults in one room and the younger people in another. Everyone shares the experiences and difficulties of living with someone who abuses alcohol, and focuses on solutions that they have found. By pointing out positive ways to cope, the members support and comfort each other. Everyone is welcome.

Many large cities have alcohol information centers sponsored by the National Council on Alcoholism that give information and guidance to the alcoholic, family, friends, and employers. If in doubt, check the phone book for local listings under "Alcoholism" or consult the list of organizations in the back of this book.

## ? ? ?
## HOW DO YOU KNOW WHEN IT'S TIME TO GO FOR HELP?

Everyone needs other people with whom they can talk over their problems, especially if the problems are about long-time, buried feelings. Uncovering these sore spots can take courage to begin and much time to continue. But the rewards can be great and long-lasting.

How do *you* know when it's time for *you* to call on a professional? This list of questions can help you decide. If you answer "Yes" to some or all of them, you should think about going for help.

*Have I lost interest in things I used to enjoy?*

*Do I have trouble keeping my mind on school-work?*

*Do I cry a lot?*

*Am I sad and depressed much of the time?*

*Do I spend a lot of my time sleeping?*

*Have I lost my appetite?*

*Am I often angry and irritable?*

*Do I sometimes think about suicide?*

*Do I feel that I have nothing to live for?*

*Have I started drinking alcohol to make myself feel good?*

107

When you meet with a counselor, a psychiatrist, a social worker, or other helping professional, you can feel free to talk about everything and anything. Drugs, lies, feelings of anger—these are just a few of the things you can discuss. All that you say is strictly confidential. This kind of help is based on trust: you trust the therapist not to repeat anything you say; he or she trusts you to be as honest as possible.

But getting into treatment is not enough. Treatment must go along with building a new life. This includes many things: finding new values and skills; discovering new ways of handling feelings; thinking less about yourself and more about others; putting an end to the lies and denial that are part of alcoholic behavior; breaking up friendships with people who drink and making new friends.

Depression, anger, and self-pity are common emotions in families of alcoholics and can slow recovery for the alcoholic. Members react to the alcoholic's problems by feeling sad and unhappy. Many feel sorry for themselves and are unable to take care of their daily activities. Facing and overcoming these negative feelings can make everyone stronger and surer of themselves and their abilities.

# SOURCE NOTES

**CHAPTER 1**

1. U.S. Congress, Senate Subcommittee on Children, Families, Drugs and Alcoholism, *Hearing*, May 12, 1987, p. 5.
2. Ibid., p. 5.
3. Ibid., p. 5.
4. Martha Sheehan, "Survey Reveals High Rate of Exposure to Alcoholism," *Recovery Press*, December 1991, p. 3.
5. National Clearinghouse for Alcohol and Drug Information, *Children of Alcoholics, Facts and Figures*, (Rockville, MD, 1987).
6. Ibid.
7. Sheehan, p. 3.

**CHAPTER 2**

1. U.S. Department of Health and Human Services, *Seventh Special Report to the U.S. Congress on Alcohol and Health*, January 1990, p. xxi.
2. Ibid.
3. Ibid., p. ix.
4. National Council on Alcoholism and Drug Dependence, *Youth and Alcohol: A National Survey* (Washington, DC, 14 June 1991).
5. National Council on Alcoholism and Drug Dependence, *Alcoholism: FYI* (Washington, DC, September 1991).
6. Ibid.
7. U.S. Department of Health and Human Services, Office for Substance Abuse Prevention, *What's Important about Children of Alcoholics* (no date given).
8. Ibid.

9. Felicity Barringer, "With Teens and Alcohol, It's Just Say When," *New York Times,* 23 June 1991, sec. 4. p. 1.
10. U.S. Department of Health and Human Services, Seventh Special Report to the U.S. Congress on January 1990, *Alcohol and Health*, p. 29.
11. Ibid., p. 30.
12. Ibid., p. 31.
13. Ibid., p. 31.
14. Ibid., p. 34.
15. Ibid., p. 34.

**CHAPTER 3**

1. National Council on Alcoholism and Drug Dependence, *Fact Sheet: Alcoholism and Alcohol-Related Problems* (Washington, DC, revised November 1990).
2. Ibid.
3. National Council on Alcoholism and Drug Dependence, *Fact Sheet: Alcohol-Related Birth Defects* (Washington, DC, revised March 1990).
4. National Council on Alcoholism and Drug Dependence, *Fact Sheet: Alcoholism and Alcohol-Related Problems* (Washington, DC, revised November 1990).
5. Ibid.
6. Ibid.
7. U.S. Department of Health and Human Services, *Seventh Special Report to the U.S. Congress on Alcohol and Health,* January 1990, p. 91.
8. Ibid.
9. Don Pratt, "Sponsoring the Suicidal Alcoholic," *Recovery Press*, February 1992, p. 12.
10. Daniel Goleman, "As Addiction Medicine Gains, Experts Debate What It Should Cover," *New York Times*, 31 March 1992, sec. C, p. 3.
11. National Institute on Alcohol Abuse and Alcoholism, *Fetal Alcohol Syndrome*, No. 13, PH 297, July 1991.
12. National Council on Alcoholism and Drug Dependence, *Fact Sheet: Alcohol-Related Birth Defects* (Washington, DC, revised March 1990).

13. "Doctors Criticized on Fetal Problem," *New York Times*, 11 December 1990, sec. B, p. 10.
14. Stan J. Katz, M.D. and Aimee E. Liu, *The Co-Dependency Conspiratory* (New York: Warner, 1991), p. 20.

**CHAPTER 4**

1. National Clearinghouse for Alcohol and Drug Information, *Children of Alcoholics, Facts and Figures* (Rockville, MD, 1987).
2. Ibid.
3. U.S. Department of Health and Human Services, *Seventh Special Report to the U.S. Congress on Alcohol and Health*, January 1990, p. 5.
4. Daniel Goleman, " 'Wisdom' on Alcoholic's Child Called Stuff of Fortune Cookies," *New York Times*, 19 February 1992, sec. C, p. 12.
5. National Council on Alcoholism and Drug Dependence, *Fact Sheet: Youth and Alcohol* (Washington, DC, June 1990).

**CHAPTER 5**

1. U.S. Department of Health and Human Services, Office for Substance Abuse Prevention, *What's Important about Children of Alcoholics* (no date given).
2. Marc Galanter, ed., *Recent Developments in Alcoholism, Vol. 9, Children of Alcoholics* (New York: Plenum Press, 1991), p. 263.
3. Ibid.
4. U.S. Congress, Senate Subcommittee on Children, Families, Drugs and Alcoholism, *Hearing*, May 12, 1987, p. 5
5. U.S. Department of Health and Human Services, *Seventh Special Report to the U.S. Congress on Alcohol and Health*, January 1990, p. 5.
6. National Institute on Alcohol Abuse and Alcoholism, *Alcohol Alert*, No. 9, PH 288, July 1990 (unpaged).
7. Ibid.
8. Christina Parker, *Children of Alcoholics: Growing Up Unheard* (Din Publications, Phoenix, AZ, March 1986) (unpaged).
9. U.S. Congress, Senate Subcommittee on Children, Families, Drugs and Alcoholism, *Hearing*, May 12, 1987, p. 5.

**CHAPTER 6**

1. Martha Sheehan, "Survey Reveals High Rate of Exposure to Alcoholism," *Recovery Press*, December 1991, p. 3.
2. National Council on Alcoholism and Drug Dependence, *Fact Sheet: Alcoholism, Other Drug Addictions and Related Problems Among Women*, (Washington, DC, revised June 1990) (unpaged).
3. U.S. Department of Health and Human Services, Office for Substance Abuse Prevention, *What's Important about Children of Alcoholics* (no date given).
4. U.S. Congress, Senate Subcommittee on Children, Families, Drugs and Alcoholism, *Hearing*, May 12, 1987, p. 12.
5. Ibid.
6. Claudia Black, *Double Duty* (New York: Ballantine, 1990), p. 5.
7. Daniel Goleman, " 'Wisdom' on Alcoholic's Child Called Stuff of Fortune Cookies," *New York Times*, 19 February 1992, sec. C, p. 12.

**CHAPTER 7**

1. National Council on Alcoholism and Drug Dependence, *Alcoholism in the Family* (Washington, DC, 1991 October 4) (unpaged).
2. Ibid.
3. Claudia Black, *Double Duty* (New York: Ballantine, 1990), p. 88.
4. Daniel Goleman, "Family Rituals May Promote Better Adjustment," *New York Times*, 11 March 1992, sec. C, p. 14.
5. National Council on Alcoholism and Drug Dependence, *Alcoholism in the Family* (Washington, DC, 4 October 1991) (unpaged).
6. Marc, Galanter, ed., *Recent Developments in Alcoholism, Vol. 9, Children of Alcoholics* (New York: Plenum Press, 1991), p. 328.
7. National Clearinghouse for Alcohol and Drug Information, *Children of Alcoholics, Facts and Figures*, (Rockville, MD, 1987).
8. Marc Galanter, ed., p. 328.
9. Daniel Goleman, " 'Wisdom' on Alcoholic's Child Called

Stuff of Fortune Cookies,'' *New York Times*, 19 February 1992, sec. C, p. 12.

## CHAPTER 8

1. National Council on Alcoholism and Drug Dependence, *Fact Sheet: Alcoholism and Alcohol-Related Problems* (Washington, DC, revised November 1990).
2. Ibid.
3. Ibid.
4. U.S. Department of Health and Human Services, *The Third Triennial Report to Congress, Drug Abuse and Drug Abuse Research*, 1991, p. 332.
5. Ibid., p. 39.
6. U.S. Department of Health and Human Services, *Seventh Special Report to the U.S. Congress on Alcohol and Health*, January 1990, p. 210.
7. Ibid., p. 212.
8. Ibid., p. 213.
9. Ibid., p. 223.
10. National Council on Alcoholism and Drug Dependence, *Fact Sheet: Youth and Alcohol* (Washington, DC, June 1990).

## CHAPTER 9

1. National Institute on Alcohol Abuse and Alcoholism, Alcohol Alert Supplement, *Advances in Alcoholism Treatment and Research*, No. 13, PH 297, July 1991.
2. National Council on Alcoholism and Drug Dependence, *Fact Sheet: Alcoholism and Alcohol-Related Problems* (Washington, DC, revised November 1990).
3. U.S. Department of Health and Human Services, Seventh Special Report to the U.S. Congress on January 1990, *Alcohol and Health*, p. 261.
4. Ibid., p. 269.
5. Daniel Goleman, ''Researchers Pinpoint Brain Irregularities Among Drug Addicts,'' *New York Times*, 26 June 1990, sec. C, p. 5.

# FOR FURTHER
# INFORMATION

## ASSOCIATIONS
Adult Children of
  Alcoholics (ACOA)
P.O. Box 3216
Torrance, CA 90505
213-534-1815

Al-Anon/Alateen
P.O. Box 862
Midtown Station
New York, NY 10018
1-800-356-9996

Alcoholics Anonymous (AA)
15 E. 26th Street, Rm 1810
New York, NY 10010
212-683-3900

American Council for
  Drug Education
204 Monroe Street
Suite 110
Rockville, MD 20850
301-294-0600

Children of Alcoholics
  Foundation
P.O. Box 4185
Grand Central Station
New York, NY 10163-4185
212-754-0656

Coalition of Hispanic Health
  and Human Services
  Organizations (COSSMHO)
1030 15th Street, NW
Suite 1053
Washington, DC 20005
202-387-5000

Families Anonymous, Inc.
P.O. Box 548
Van Nuys, CA 91408
818-989-7841

Institute on Black Chemical
  Abuse
2614 Nicollet Avenue
Minneapolis, MN 55408
612-871-7878

Just Say No Foundation
1777 North California Blvd.
Room 210
Walnut Creek, CA 94596

Mothers Against Drunk
  Driving
511 E. John Carpenter
  Freeway
Suite 700
Irving, TX 75062

National Association for
Children of Alcoholics
(NACOA)
31582 Coast Highway
Suite B
South Laguna, CA 92677
714-499-3889

National Association for
Native American Children
of Alcoholics (NANOCOA)
P.O. Box 18736
Seattle, WA 98118
206-322-5601

National Black Alcoholism
and Addictions Council
1629 K Street, NW
Suite 802
Washington, DC 20006
202-296-2696

National Clearinghouse for
Alcohol and Drug
Information (NCADI)
P.O. Box 2345
Rockville, MD 20852
1-800-729-6686

National Council on
Alcoholism
and Drug Dependence
1511 K Street, NW
Washington, DC 20005
1-800-NCA-CALL

Rational Recovery Systems
P. O. Box 800
Lotus, CA 95651
916-621-4374

SOS (Secular Organizations
for Sobriety)
P. O. Box 5
Buffalo, NY 14215
716-834-2922

Women for Sobriety
P.O. Box 618
Quakertown, PA 18951
215-536-8026

**FOR INFORMATION ON STUDENT
ASSISTANCE PROGRAMS:**

National Organization on
Student Assistance
Programs
250 Arapahoe, Suite 301
Boulder, CO 80302
1-800-972-4636

Student Assistance Services
300 Farm Road
Ardsley, NY 10502
1-800-999-1199

# BIBLIOGRAPHY

**BOOKS ON ALCOHOLISM
AND REACHING OUT**

Brooks, Cathleen. *The Secret Everyone Knows*. San Diego, CA: The Kroc Foundation, 1981.

Black, Claudia. *My Dad Loves Me, My Dad Has a Disease*. Denver, CO: Medical Administration Company, 1982.

Culin, Charlotte. *Cages of Glass, Flowers of Time*. Scarsdale, NY: Bradbury Press, 1979. Ages 12–16.

Cermak, Timmen. *Evaluating and Treating Adult Children of Alcoholics*. San Francisco, CA: Johnson Institute, 1991.

Figueroa, Ronaldo. *El Secreto de Pablito*. Pompano Beach, FL: Health Communications, 1984. Ages 7–12.

Hammond, Mary and Chestnut, Lynnann. *My Mom Doesn't Look Like an Alcoholic*. Pompano Beach, FL: Health Communications, 1986. Ages 7–12.

Hornick, Edith. *You and Your Alcoholic Parent*. New York: Association Press, 1974. Ages 11–16.

Mazer, Harry. *The War on Villa Street*. New York: Dell, 1978. Ages 12–14.

Norris, Gunilla. *Take my Walking Slow*. New York: Atheneum, 1970. Ages 5–8.

Sher, Kenneth. *Children of Alcoholics: A Critical Appraisal of Theory and Research*. Chicago, IL: University of Chicago Press, 1991.

Seixas, Judith S., *Alcohol—What It Is, What It Does*. New York: Greenwillow Books, 1974.

———. *Living with a Parent Who Drinks Too Much*. New York: Greenwillow Books, 1979.

Stanck, Muriel. *Don't Hurt Me Mama*. Albert Whitman, 1983. Ages 5–8.

Williams, Mary. *My Precious Child*. Pompano Beach, FL: Health Communications, 1991.

117

# INDEX

119

121

# ABOUT THE AUTHOR

Gilda Berger is a former teacher of special education who is now a full-time writer of books for children and young adults. She has authored many books for Franklin Watts, including *Drug Abuse: The Impact on Society, Smoking Not Allowed, Violence and Drugs, Mental Illness, Violence and the Family*, and most recently, *Addiction*, Revised Edition. She is married to author Melvin Berger. They have two daughters and three grandsons.